intermittent

Fasting

for women over 5͞8

TABLE OF CONTENTS

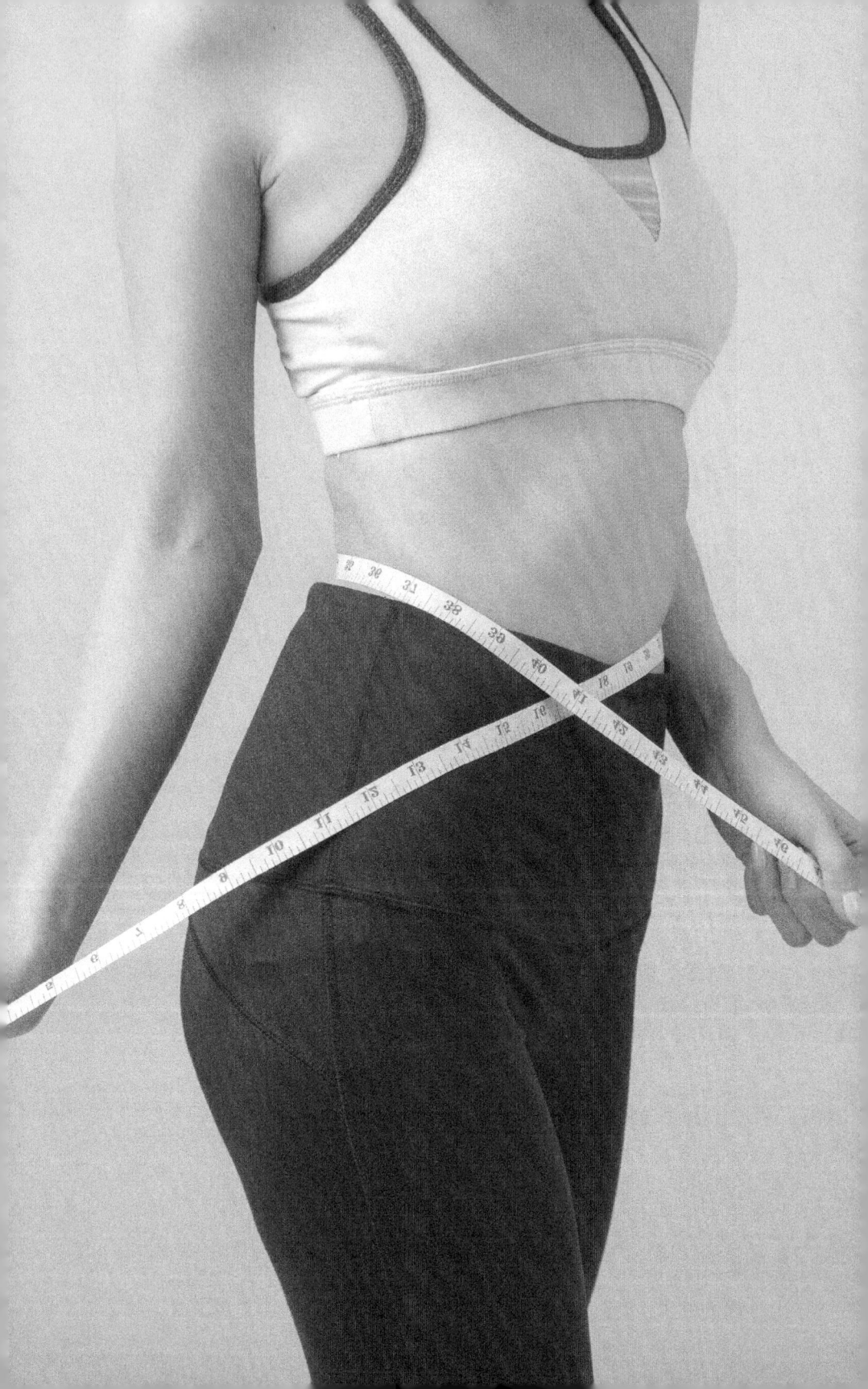

INTRODUCTION

The 50s can be the point where you come across many such issues and may not be able to understand the correct strategy to navigate easily. Intermittent fasting is one of the best ways for women to find ways into good health in their 50s. It is easy to follow, effective, and a very efficient way to stay healthy and fit.

Losing weight is easier with intermittent fasting, as it can help you in reaching ketosis fast. You will not only lose weight but you will also be able to burn the adamant belly fat.

Intermittent fasting is also a savior for women over 50, as it can help in initiating autophagy. This is the process that can bring amazing anti-aging properties and support your body from within during long-standing allergies, immunity issues, and chronic inflammations.

From various intermittent fasting protocols specifically suitable for women over 50 to the ways through which initiating ketosis and autophagy will be easy, this book will cover everything in vivid detail.

Every claim in this book will have an explanation so that you can understand if that can work for you or not.

Many things that make weight loss more difficult after age 50 include; decreased appetite, achy joints, diminished muscle mass, and even sleep problems. At the same time, losing weight, particularly dangerous belly fat, will lower the chance of your health problems.

Naturally, the risk of developing many diseases increases as you age. In some cases, when it comes to weight loss and reducing the chance of developing usually age-related diseases, intermittent fasting for women over 50 may act as a virtual youth pool.

So, take your time and enjoy it!

CHAPTER 1

WHAT IS INTERMITTENT FASTING AND HOW IT CAME ABOUT

Basically, fasting is defined as abstaining from eating anything. It is the deliberate action of depriving the body of any form of food for more than six hours.

Whereas intermittent fasting is a nutritional strategy that provides for a more or less long interval of fasting over a few days, alternating with a period in which you can take food without being too enslaved to the weights but still taking into account some precautions. This regimen does not need to be carried out every day, but you can choose the different ways suitable for your goals and lifestyle.

During the hours of feeding, it is possible to consume almost all foods giving preference to low-calorie foods such as meat, fish, eggs, limiting simple sugars, and choosing those with a low glycemic index, bread, pasta, and rice possibly whole grains, legumes, dried and fresh fruits, and good fats.

One of its forms is where the fast is carried out cyclically to reduce the overall caloric intake in a day.

The main goal is to divert the body's attention from the digestion of food. During the fasting period, in fact, a series of metabolic changes take place in the body: since there is no food left in the stomach to digest, the body focuses on the process of recovery and maintenance.

To most people, it may sound unhealthy and damaging to the body, but scientific research has proven that fasting can produce positive results for the human mind and body. According to Healthline, the American medical-scientific journal, this system helps reduce overall calorie intake and as a result not only can help people lose weight effortlessly but can also improve the overall functioning of metabolism. It can also positively affect our minds by teaching self-discipline and fighting against bad eating practices and habits. It is basically an umbrella term that is used to define all voluntary forms of fasting. This dietary approach does not restrict the consumption of certain food items; rather, it works by reducing the overall food intake, leaving enough space to meet the essential nutrients the body needs. Therefore, it is proven to be far more effective and much easier to implement, given that the dieter completely understands the nature and science of intermittent fasting.

Intermittent fasting is categorized into three broad methods of food abstinence, including alternate-day fasting, daily restrictions, and periodic fasting. The means may vary, but the end goal of it remains the same, which is to achieve a better metabolism, healthy body weight, and active lifestyle. The American Heart Association, AHA, has also studied intermittent fasting and its results. According to the AHA, it can help in countering insulin resistance, cardio metabolic diseases, and leads to weight loss. However, a question mark remains on the sustainability of this health-effective method. The 2019 research "Effects of intermittent fasting on health, aging, and disease" has also found it to be effective against insulin resistance, inflammation, hypertension, obesity, and dyslipidemia. However, the work on this dietary approach is still underway, and the traditional methods of fasting which existed for almost the entire human history, in every religion from Buddhism to Jainism, Orthodox Christianity, Hinduism, and Islam, are studied to found relevance in today's age of science and technology.

How Does It Work

Eating is a primary need that we satisfy unceasingly from birth. Every day we introduce food into our organisms. When we eat, the metabolism activates itself to start the digestive process.

When we fast, however, we stop this process and this energy dispensing. The saved energy is thus diverted to other metabolic processes, essentially of a restorative type.

Dr. Longo, Director of the Institute of Longevity at the University of Southern California, explained how thanks to this practice: "the immune system frees itself from useless, unnecessary cells, while it is driven to put back into action naturally, as was the case at the moments of birth and growth, stem cells capable of ensuring regeneration."

The body not engaged in food digestion can better devote itself to its purification by moving toxins away through its emunctory organs. These large internal cleanings obviously have positive repercussions on the state of health of organs and tissues. The organism is detoxified and revitalized.

American researchers at Yale's School of Medicine highlighted how during the break from food, our organism produces a substance capable of extinguishing chronic inflammation. It is called the β-hydroxybutyrate (BHB) and it is capable of converting into a complex set of proteins that guide the inflammatory response in many pathologies, including several autoimmune diseases. A good result suggests how therapeutic fasting can be used in the early treatment of many inflammatory-based diseases in the future.

In fact, it works between alternating periods of eating and fasting. It is a much more flexible approach, as there are many options to choose from according to body type, size, weight goals, and nutritional needs.

The human body works like a synchronized machine that requires sufficient time for self-healing and repair. When we constantly eat junk and unhealthy food or too high a quantity of food without the consideration of our caloric needs, it leads to obesity and toxic build-up in the body. That is why fasting comes as a natural means of detoxifying the body and giving it enough time to utilize its fat stores.

Whatever the human body consumes is ultimately broken into glucose, which is later utilized by the cells in glycolysis to release energy. Intermittent fasting seems to reverse this process by deliberately creating energy deprivation, which is then fulfilled by breaking down the existing fat stores.

Intermittent fasting works through lipolysis; though it is a natural body process, it can only be initiated when the blood glucose levels drop to a sufficiently low point. That point can be achieved through fasting and exercising. When a person cuts off the external glucose supply for several hours, the body switches to lipolysis. This process of breaking the fats also releases other by-products like ketones that are capable of reducing the oxidative stress of the body and helping in its detoxification.

Mark Mattson, a neuroscientist from Johns Hopkins Medicine University, has studied intermittent fasting for almost 25 years of his career. He laid out the workings of this dietary approach by clarifying its clinical application and the science behind it. According to him, it must be pursued for a healthy lifestyle.

While discussing the application of this dietary approach, it is imperative to understand how intermittent fasting stands out from casual dieting practices. It is not mere abstinence from eating. What is eaten in this dietary lifestyle is equally important as the fasting itself. It does not result in malnutrition; rather, it promotes healthy eating along with the fast. Intermittent fasting is divided into two different states that follow one another. The cycle starts with the "FED" state, which is followed by a "Fasting" state. The duration of the fasting state and the frequency of the FED state are established by the method of intermittent fasting. The latter is characterized by high blood glucose levels, whereas during the fasting state the body goes through a gradual decline in glucose levels. This decline in glucose signals the pancreas and the brain to meet the body's energy needs by processing the available fat molecules. However, if the fasting state is followed by a FED state in which a person binge eats food rich in carbs and fats, it will turn out to be more hazardous for their health. Therefore, the fasting period must be accompanied by a healthy diet.

The Science Behind Intermittent Fasting

Biologically, it works at many levels, from cellular levels to gene expression and body growth. To understand the science behind the workings of intermittent fasting, it is important to learn about the role of insulin levels, human growth hormones, cellular repair, and gene expression. Intermittent fasting firstly lowers glucose levels, which in turn drops insulin levels. This lowering of insulin helps fat burning in the body, thus gradually curbing obesity and related disorders. Controlled levels of insulin are also responsible for preventing diabetes and insulin resistance. On the other hand, intermittent fasting boosts the production of human growth hormones up to five times. The increased production of HGH aids quick fat burning and muscle formation.

During the fasting state, the body goes into the process of self-healing at cellular levels, thus removing the unwanted and non-functional cells and debris. This creates a cleansing effect that directly or indirectly nourishes the body and allows it to grow under reduced oxidative stress. Likewise, fasting even affects the gene expression within the human body. The cell functions according to the coding and decoding of the gene's expression; when this transcription occurs at a normal pace in a healthy environment, it automatically translates into the longevity of the cells, and fasting ensures unhindered transcription. Thus, intermittent fasting fights aging and cancer and boosts the immune system by strengthening the body cells.

The Practice of Fasting Through the Course of Human History

Fasting is an ancient tradition and time-tested approach. It is one of the best tools to lose weight. It also improves concentration, prevents Alzheimer's, extends life, controls insulin resistance levels, and reverses the aging process. It is not a new concept. People have just forgotten it. Everything we eat increases the level of insulin to a certain extent. Eating healthy foods prevents those high levels. Some food items are much better than others, but they all still increase the level of insulin. The only key to averting resistance levels is to sustain low insulin levels. If they all raise insulin levels, then voluntary abstinence is the best answer, i.e., fasting.

The practice of fasting has therapeutically been used since the 5th century B.C., when Hippocrates, a Greek physician, suggested abstinence from drink or food for his patients who had certain symptoms of an illness. Some called it fasting; others believed that patients naturally lost appetite in certain diseases. Some people thought that managing eating levels during such conditions were unnecessary. But many people believed that fasting was an essential and natural way to recover. An in-depth understanding of fasting and its physiological effects moved towards the evolutionary road later in the 19th century—studies organized for the first time on humans and animals.

In the early 20th century, much was known and studied

about nutrition. The nutritional needs and requirements of a human body were studied in detail, and some different, new approaches to fasting emerged.

There were also some other approaches, modified fasting, which allowed an intake of 200–500 calories a day and included spiritual or psychological therapy. Depending on the form of fasting method that was being used, calories were in the shape of bread, fruit juice, honey, milk, or vegetable broth. The modified fasting approach was different from a diet having low calories that allowed a maximum of 800 calories a day. It had the primary purpose of losing weight. On the other hand, intermittent fasting involved calorie restriction in cyclic periods like 12 hours of fasting plan followed by 12 hours of regular consumption of calories.

The ancient people, especially Greeks, considered nature as a guiding force in their medical treatment. According to them, fasting was undoubtedly one of the best traditions of ancient healing in human history, and it improved the cognitive abilities of a person. Many religions and cultures have practiced it. But, keep in mind that fasting is very much different from starvation. Fasting is about voluntarily abstaining from food. Starvation, on the other hand, is an involuntary action. You probably have no control over it. People with starvation do not have the choice of deciding the time of their next meal. They do not even know if that time will ever come or not. So, do not confuse these terms.

Fasting was also supported by many intellectual giants like Philip Paracelsus, who is the father of toxicology. He considered fasting an excellent remedy, and called it the "physician within." Benjamin Franklin, who had a wide range of knowledge and intellect in various areas, also called fasting the best medicine, along with resting. Fasting has also served the spiritual purpose of many religions. Religious leaders like Buddha, Jesus Christ, and prophet Muhammed shared one common belief of considering fasting as a healing power. It is also called purification or cleansing in a spiritual context. But fasting developed differently and independently among these cultures and religions as something profound and intrinsically beneficial.

In Buddhism, people consume food just in the morning time and do fasting from noon to the next day morning. On the other hand, Muslims choose the time from the sunrise to the sunset in their holy month, Ramadan. Prophet Muhammad used to encourage fasting on other days of the week, too, except Ramadan. Fasting in Ramadan is different from other fasting protocols. The use of fluids is also forbidden during this fast. So, they include a little bit of mild dehydration in their fast too.

So, the idea of fasting has genuinely evolved. Many influential people have agreed that fasting is a truly beneficial approach to a healthy life. As discussed, fasting has a long history, but various aspects of why and how we should do have changed drastically. Modern approaches towards intermittent fasting comprise fasting periods regularly occurring in between the eating periods. You can eat healthy food. The approach is to do it by sticking to a small-time frame, the eating window, and staying away from food during the fasting window. Today, we have absolute freedom to select any form of fasting. The intermittent fast lasts from 6–24 hours for an extended period. You can go on a fast for just one day in a week, a month, or a year. You can select the shorter fast approach or, the longer one. You will not find one specific best approach to fasting. It is a very personal preference and experience. It is just simple, effective, and practical.

CHAPTER 2

50 YEARS AND THE CHANGES

Generally, 50 years is considered a turning point for our physiology and metabolism. Okay, so what's different after 50?

Your Metabolism Slows Down with Age

We can define your metabolism as all the chemical reactions that help keep your body active. A person's metabolism determines how many calories are consumed each day.

Lucky people with a faster metabolism will burn calories faster than others, gaining weight much less easily. If you are reading this book, you are probably among ordinary people with a standard or slow speed metabolism. Although measuring how fast a person's metabolism is not a simple task, there are various factors to take into consideration:

- **Resting metabolic rate (RMR):** This indicates how many calories you burn in a resting state.

- **The thermic effect of food (TEF):** Indicates how many calories you burn through absorbing and digesting food.

- **Exercise:** This indicates how many calories you burn through physical activity.

- **Non-exercise activity thermogenesis (NEAT):** Activities like walking, moving objects, and washing dishes still burn some calories. This index indicates how many calories you burn during these activities.

So, what are the main reasons why our metabolism slows down with age?

- **Less physical activity**: Physical exercise activities contribute 10% to 30% to the total calories burned daily. For some very active people, this number can reach even 50%! Unfortunately, research shows that older people tend to be less active than younger and over a quarter of Americans aged 50–65 don't do any physical activity outside work.

- **Our body is less efficient since its components are aging:** RMR is determined by two cellular components that drive chemical reactions inside our body. These components are called **mitochondria** and **sodium-potassium pumps**. According to various research papers, both components lose efficiency as we age, reducing daily burned calories.

- **As we age, we tend to lose lean muscle mass**: It has been estimated that the average adult can lose up to 8% of lean muscle mass during each decade (after 30). This process is known as **sarcopenia** and can lead to various health issues like fractures, weakness, and early death.

Sarcopenia also has the secondary effect of slowing down your metabolism since the amount of muscles mass increases your RMR. Sarcopenia happens for various reasons:

- Fewer calories and proteins are consumed during the day

- Hormone production is decreased (**Estrogen**, **Testosterone**, **Growth Hormone**)

- Reduced physical activity

Having learned some of the basics of how metabolism works, your next question might be, "Okay, how much slower is my metabolism?"

There is no easy answer; there are various research papers on the argument, and the results obtained with the multiple experiments differ enormously in some cases.

All scientists seem to agree that the RMR tends to decrease according to the age group, having found only one experiment to produce conflicting results on the subject. This latest experiment followed a group of people for decades by measuring their metabolism. It has been hypothesized that the minimal variation of RMR found during this experiment is due to the extreme longevity of some participants (over 95 years old). The underlying idea is that their unique metabolism was one of the main factors in increasing their longevity.

HGH Production Is Lower

Human Growth Hormone (HGH) is an important hormone produced by our pituitary gland, and it plays a critical role in various instances:

- Muscle growth

- Body composition

- Cell repair

- Metabolism

- Body strength

- Physical exercise performance

- Injury and diseases recovery

As you can imagine, a reduction in the production of this hormone can directly affect the quality of our life and facilitate weight gain. The scientific community believes that there is a direct correlation between HGH levels and fat mass percentage in our bodies.

After monitoring the HGH release levels of more than a thousand patients over 24 hours, a considerable decline was observed in patients with the highest belly fat percentage.

Unfortunately, the decline in HGH production is not mainly determined by body dysfunctions but most commonly by aging.

There are various ways to improve our HGH production; the most common is to start an appropriate intermittent fasting diet.

Through appropriate IF is possible to raise HGH levels by over 300% in only three days. While progressing with the diet, the levels of HGH production will continue to rise until reaching 1250% after one week. We will talk more about the IF diet in the following chapters; for now, it is essential to remember that some type of intermittent fasting is not meant for long periods and should be stopped at the most opportune moment.

Another way to increase HGH levels is assuming supplements, Arginine and GABA (Gamma-aminobutyric acid), are usually the two most popular choices. However, it is important to note that recent studies show that the best results are found while also doing physical activity. Therefore, supplements alone might not sort the desired effect.

Eating in a controlled manner can help improve HGH levels. For example, reducing the daily sugar intake will help reduce the insulin levels in our bodies. This will consequently facilitate the production of HGH.

It also plays a fundamental role when we eat our meals; having a late dinner, especially if rich in carbohydrates, will increase our insulin levels by inhibiting the nocturnal production of HGH.

It is therefore advisable to have dinner no later than 3 hours before going to bed.

HIT (High-Intensity Training) is another effective way to raise your HGH levels. Physical exercise, in general, plays a crucial role in improving your HGH production. Studies have shown that HIT is the type of exercise that has the most significant impact on HGH production.

The peak of HGH production occurs during the night when our body is at rest. We can visualize the release of HGH as pulses coordinated by our internal clock—**Circadian Rhythm.** Since most HGH is released before midnight, studies have shown that a poor sleep schedule can be one of the leading causes of the reduction of HGH levels.

Optimizing our sleep, therefore, plays a fundamental role; the perfect rest can be obtained with some simple changes in your lifestyle:

- Avoid caffeine and sugars before going to bed.

- Do relaxing activities, such as reading a book, when in bed.

- Make sure your bedroom is quiet and at a comfortable temperature.

- Avoid blue light exposure before bedtime—such as the one generated by smartphones.

With aging, it is not easy to maintain optimal levels of HGH; for this reason, it is possible to resort to various supplements that can help us in this task:

- **Creatine:** It can help increase HGH levels for 2–6 hours.

- **Glycine:** According to some studies, it can help with short-term spikes in HGH. Your doctor might suggest it to better support physical activity.

- **Glutamine:** It can help to raise HGH levels up to 80%—temporarily.

- **L-dopa:** This is used mainly for Parkinson's disease treatments and also helps to raise HGH levels.

I strongly suggest consulting a doctor before taking substances aimed at improving your HGH levels. It is always a good idea to discuss your case with a specialist to understand if you require one of these supplements and define the most appropriate dosage.

Other Effects of Aging

In this section, I would like to quickly provide an overview of the other effects of aging that impact our physical condition after 50.

Women's bones increase in density until the age of 30 but, after 35, we slowly begin to lose density due to changes in hormone levels. This process of loss of density becomes even faster after menopause. No ways have been discovered yet to stop this constant decay, but it is possible to enormously slow it down with a healthy lifestyle and regular physical activity. For prevention purposes, it is also advisable to carry out a bones density screening exam around the age of 50 to assess the situation and put into action the most appropriate remedies to fight osteoporosis years before the problem arises.

Unfortunately, heart disease rates tend to rise after menopause; this is due to the reduction in estrogen production. Estrogens help keep arteries healthy and improve **HDL** levels, also known as "**good cholesterol**," while maintaining **LDL** under control known as **"bad cholesterol."**

After menopause, the amount of estrogen in our body begins to drop, increasing the risk of cardiovascular disease by up to 300%. Fortunately, there are methods to reduce this risk considerably; a balanced diet and regular exercise are, once again, our primary weapons in the fight against aging. In addition, intermittent fasting is a perfect method to reset our bodies and reduce the amount of LDL.

Unfortunately, you may have already noticed that aging does not even spare our skin and hair. Our skin begins to lose its elasticity after the age of 40, and some annoying wrinkles start to appear. In addition, our hair becomes finer, less resistant, and prone to graying. Some of you may have noticed your first white hair already around the age of 30, while others, many years later. The graying of the hair is directly related to our genes, and it is a process that varies enormously from person to person. For all the effects not directly related to our genes, there are numerous ways to slow down the effects of aging but there is no magic formula other than diet, physical training, and supplements.

As a woman reaches her forties and fifties, she goes through menopause; her hormones gradually decrease as her ovaries stop producing estrogen and progesterone, preventing menstruation. She is said to have entered menopause because she has not had a cycle for 12 months, but amenorrhea isn't the only symptom of menopause.

After menopause, women may become less receptive to

insulin, as if the other signs weren't enough. As a result, they may have difficulty absorbing sugar and processed carbohydrates; this physiologic transition is known as insulin resistance, associated with fatigue, sleep difficulties, and weight gain.

As you will soon discover in your body, intermittent fasting is one of the most powerful allies we have in fighting the signs of aging; it is not only valuable for losing weight but

CHAPTER 3

WHO IS THE INTERMITTENT FASTING FOR

also to reset our organism.

Intermittent fasting is tailored to most types of individuals but excludes children, pregnant or breastfeeding women, anyone with current or previous eating disorders, those who take medication and are advised to refrain from skipping meals, and a list of other health conditions that will be discussed below.

Before starting any new diet or incorporating new weight loss methods, it is necessary to always consult your medical physician first. Although intermittent fasting is not necessarily considered a diet, it does fall under some of the most effective weight loss methods on the market today.

This dietary approach is idealized as one of the easiest weight loss solutions out there today, there are a few downsides that you have to consider, which is yet another reason why it is vital to consult your medical practitioner before starting it.

Who Can Fast?

Intermittent fasting has numerous effects on the body, all of which are most beneficial, and if you're one of the lucky people that can last for 14 to 24 hours at a time, you will reap those benefits. The truth is, almost anyone can fast, particularly someone that has a clean bill of health. Healthy adults are the most likely to only benefit from it and not experience any side effects or have a bad time practicing it.

Since starting doesn't require you to follow a crazy meal plan or go to extreme measures to achieve your goals, it is especially appealing for those who have struggled to lose weight or possibly can't exercise. It also presents itself as an impeccable weight loss option for people with disabilities and health issues.

If you take a person that has been diagnosed with obesity, for instance, he/she is unlikely to be motivated enough to start working out. They may feel defeated and like the only option they have is to give up on their health and weight loss goals, which is why intermittent fasting is the perfect option for them.

It is just as good of an option for anyone who has been diagnosed with long-term health issues, including type 1 and type 2 diabetes, hypertension, cardiovascular diseases, inflammatory diseases, high cholesterol, and irregular blood sugar levels. The dietary practice has been linked to relieving symptoms related to these health issues and in some cases, even supporting the recovery of patients and curing them. Intermittent fasting is also great for cancer patients undergoing chemotherapy and has been linked to reducing symptoms of feeling sick caused by the therapy (Pattillo, 2019).

Other than healthy individuals and people diagnosed with health issues that can benefit from intermittent fasting, it is important to highlight that men have a much better experience with this dietary practice than women. So, if you're a non-pregnant or breastfeeding woman, it is especially recommended that you consult your doctor before integrating this eating pattern into your daily routine.

Who Can't Fast?

Pregnant or Breastfeeding Women

Women who are pregnant are not allowed to fast as it can affect the growth of their baby, resulting in nutrient deficiencies and more susceptibility to infection and illnesses once born, which could affect a baby's entire life and wellbeing. During pregnancy, a woman is responsible to nourish both herself and her baby, which means she should be consuming more food, not less. This is necessary to help a baby gain a healthy weight, to provide him/her with optimal nutrition for brain and body development, as well as to develop fat stores that will help a woman in breastfeeding once a baby is born. Women are also not allowed to fast when breastfeeding as any indication of malnourishment in a woman's body could trigger a lack of milk production and even prevent lactation altogether. Eating a healthy, balanced, and nutrient-rich diet during pregnancy is just as important when breastfeeding, as you are still providing the only source of nutrients to your baby.

Nutrient-Deficiencies

Anyone with nutrient deficiencies should consult their doctor before integrating intermittent fasting into their diet and should also refrain from fasting for long periods at a time. Not supplementing your body with enough nutrients, especially those you are deficient in, could harm your body and cause symptoms of weakness, fatigue, impaired concentration, and a lack of energy in the body. Anyone with a nutrient deficiency should follow a healthy, balanced, and structured diet, and refrain from cutting out meals or food groups altogether.

Eating Disorders

Since eating disorders go hand in hand with mental illnesses, a person who has a bad relationship with food should not be advised to skip a meal or fast for long periods at a time. Even though intermittent fasting is generally good for the body, you also need a healthy mind to commit to the practice and only integrate it into your daily routine with the right intentions. The intention should never be to harm your body or to recover from any guilt you may experience from eating food.

Auto-Immune and Chronic Stress Disorders

Intermittent fasting can be good and bad for patients with auto-immune disorders. On the beneficial side, it can repair leaky gut, help initiate autophagy, reduce inflammation, boost ketogenesis, and improve the immune system. On a negative note, that is not the case with all patients. If you are a woman experiencing hormonal imbalances, adrenal fatigue, or thyroid problems, you should refrain from fasting. For these reasons, entering a state of ketosis with the ketogenic diet combined with intermittent fasting is also dangerous for the body, as it can place stress on the adrenal glands, which could worsen your auto-immune condition. Anyone with an auto-immune disorder that cannot manage stress or has been diagnosed with a chronic stress disorder is also at risk for experiencing similar complications. If you have an auto-immune disorder, you should first contact your doctor before attempting to make any changes to your diet.

Sleep Disorders

Practicing intermittent fasting can help people fall asleep and sleep more soundly, but for anyone with sleep disorders, it can be the complete opposite. People who have been diagnosed with sleep disorders shouldn't engage in intermittent fasting, as it can decrease REM sleep. People affected by sleep disorders may also struggle to sleep even more at night due to their brains being too focused on hunger, which could disrupt inconsistent sleeping patterns even more.

Type 1 and Type 2 Diabetes

As a diabetic, whether you're type 1 or type 2, you know by now that you shouldn't be skipping meals and that everything you ingest or don't ingest has an effect on your body's blood sugar levels. Well, even though intermittent fasting can be good for diabetics and even help them recover from diabetes, it can also have a negative effect on certain patients. It may cause you to feel irritable and drowsy or even give you a headache, which is your body's response to not receiving enough nutrients. Diabetics can fast but should fast with caution and only under the supervision of their doctor. If intermittent fasting is affecting your blood sugar levels, causing it to drop instead of remaining stable, you can't fast.

Gastroesophageal Reflux Disease (GERD)

Depending on the severity of your diagnosis, GERD can either reduce the symptoms of acid reflux or aggravate them. Before you incorporate intermittent fasting into your daily life, you should first consult your doctor. You should also refrain from eating spicy or acidic foods, dairy, and bread when changing your diet to support GERD.

CHAPTER 4

HOW LONG YOU CAN DO INTERMITTENT FASTING

How long you can fast is really up to you. Your body may not handle a long fast at first because it is not used to it. It will freak out, and you will not know how to respond to hunger pangs. As a result, you will break your fast before you are meant to and minimize results. Start small and make your fasts longer as you feel ready.

It is possible to fast for several days without issues. But if you feel lightheaded, you may need to break your fast. This lightheadedness is typically a symptom of low blood glucose, meaning your body is not able to sustain itself anymore.

Read on to learn about the different types of fasting and how they work. Be sure to pick the one that works for your schedule. You may not want to be fasting on a weekend when your family has a barbecue, for instance. Or if you have dinner with your family every night, be sure to pick a fast that allows having an eating window during dinner. Customize fasts so that they work for you. That is how to be successful in this approach. Otherwise, you will get frustrated and quit if you pick a fast that is too hard for you or that cuts into your life too much.

Longer Fasts—Risks and Benefits

The benefits of longer fasts are that they show better results in shorter windows of time. While it might take a year before you see results from a 12-hour fast, you will see results from a 60-hour fast on the day that you complete the fast.

But these longer fasts are much harder to do if your mind is not yet trained to accept hunger and ignore cravings. You are far more likely to crash and then binge. You must work up to these longer fasts.

These longer fasts can also interfere with your lifestyle. If you go on a long fast once a month, you will find it harder to skip or avoid major events where food is involved. You will be more tempted by food as well.

The symptoms also become stronger in these longer fasts. You will suffer from more constipation, cold, fatigue, headaches, and other unpleasant sensations. You will be hit with more cravings and hunger pangs. All of these things can make you want to give up on the fast. If you work up to it, however, these symptoms will be less noticeable, and you can work through them.

CHAPTER 5

THE RIGHT MINDSET FOR INTERMITTENT FASTING

A healthy and happy attitude is critical for a woman to keep her sanity and live a full life post-menopause. Bring those not-so-nice thoughts out into the open with these five tips on how to stay happy after menopause, including accepting the hormonal changes that come with this stage of life, taking care of your health, and keeping up an active lifestyle.

Accept Your Body's Natural Aging Process

There are certain things you can't stop or change, such as wrinkles or graying hair. Some women may be upset with the appearance of dry skin, weak nails, and thinning hair. If you compare your new look to what you had when you were younger, it's natural to feel some concerns or worry when a few shortcomings are brought to attention. However, accepting these changes as they happen more easily prevents these self-doubts.

Take Care of Your Health

You must keep exercising and make sure that you get enough sleep each night. You might not feel like going to the gym and working out, but it can be beneficial to do so. You might also begin taking vitamins and minerals, which will provide you with the nutrients you need. It can minimize the level of stress on your body and help prevent illness.

Do Something Active Every Day, Every Week, and Every Month

If you were an athlete throughout your life, you can't slow down when menopause begins. As a result, you must keep an active lifestyle to prevent muscle mass and bone mass loss. If the thought of sitting down all day sounds threatening, you should consider becoming a jogger or a swimmer. You can do other things, such as gardening or taking walks, that will help keep your heart healthy while keeping yourself fit and trim.

Eat Well and Make Good Choices

Most women go through the menopause stage with no health issues and can remain active throughout this period. However, more than 60% of women experience hot flashes and night sweats during this stage. It could be attributed to hormonal imbalances.

The most important thing you can do for your health is to take care of your weight and control your caloric intake. It is essential because it will keep you healthy and help slow down the aging process. If you are not careful about the calories you eat, the chances are that you will gain weight. You tend to lose muscle and get fat as you grow older. It means that the number on the scale could go up if you are not careful about your caloric intake.

Stay Mentally Active

There are many activities that you can do to stay mentally active. You can continue reading books, attending lectures, writing in a journal, or writing on a blog, Facebook, or Twitter about things you like and what is important to you. These activities will help keep your mind sharp and keep your brain fit and your body.

If you're a woman and post-menopausal, chances are you've been told that you need to be on hormone replacement therapy (HRT). You might still have difficulty enjoying life without hormones, but there are tricks to make it more enjoyable. So, let's take a look.

The first thing to do is work on your attitude about menopause. Don't dwell on it, even if that's what your friends do. Talk about your feelings, but don't engage in the negativity. Being a harmful individual is no longer about your age; it's more about your life attitude. You might want to have a "non-negativity club" and make it fun to meet once a week. Perhaps go out for lunch or dinner and have an enjoyable time with others going through the same things you are. Also, you may want friends over 50 in your life and invite them to a dinner or movie in your home.

You can also try to focus on the positive things about

menopause. What are you looking forward to? The extra time you have to spend with your grandchildren, a trip you'll take soon, or the fact that you'll be able to devote more time to yourself? Even if health issues arise for yourself, it's still better than staying in bed.

Always remember that as women age, we don't go through menopause; we change into women. So, some menopausal changes and experiences can be fun. Yes, you will have different menopausal symptoms, like hot flashes and mood swings, but it's not the end of your life. Ask yourself what you're going to do about it. The more you talk about not having positive thoughts about your future, the unhappier you'll make your life. Choose to be happy!

CHAPTER 6

STAGES OF INTERMITTENT FASTING

The use of short-term fasting has had a significant effect on specific hormones linked to weight loss and weight control. The purpose of intermittent fasting is to use meal timing to control, and use, mechanisms of fat burning already present in your body.

It covers the factors of metabolism, hormones, blood sugar, and other weight loss.

While most diets concentrate on material and calories, when you eat and when you don't, the most important aspect of intermittent fasting is.

The intermittent fasting stages define the metabolic process your body is going through during the periods of fasting and feeding.

Perhaps intermittent fasting is best described as a nutritional technique, aimed at losing weight. Characteristics are the fasting and feeding periods. As we are used to, it's not a diet, but finding an ideal time to eat. That puts your body through various metabolic states.

Nutritionists have been against this approach for many years, as it poses many threats to the human body. Not everybody can openly use the technique, preferably under an expert's supervision.

They now know, however, with experience over time, that the benefits are impressive, and that this food program is worth implementing. The metabolic effect of alternating foods is obvious and beneficial if we know and make the most of each of their stages.

Hypoglycemic Stage

The secret to intermittent fasting is the eating stop point. The body initially uses the stores of glucose in the liver and muscles to circulate through the blood.

You will experience other symptoms like depression as your blood glucose levels drop, dizziness, or drowsiness. Our body must attempt to escape this condition from glycogen and new glucose production.

If glycogen isn't enough, we'll secrete some other hormones to boost energy production, such as cortisol and adrenaline. Typically, once we get used to the fasting sporadic, the symptoms generally decrease.

Ketogenic Stage

That may be the secret to intermittent fasting. The body has consumed the glucose at this point; both are circulating and being retained in the liver and glycogen muscles. It opts for other energy sources.

Energy continues to be derived from fat, after specific stages of metabolism in the liver. This causes some of the ketone bodies known as by-products. These help to continue our functions as a substrate but also have direct and indirect effects on our bodies.

That's the secret to losing weight. We take energy from fat and burn it at an excellent rate.

Lifestyle Stage

It is a time for rejoicing! You'll be feeling so good about yourself by this time. You wear prettier clothes; people complement you both left and right. Above all, you're feeling so good!

You'll be counting macronutrients at this stage. Macros for macronutrients are short and are the type of food in a human diet. This consists of carbohydrates, calcium, and fat. All of these matters are important for the human body.

Final Stage

The last stage has to do with adjusting to the occasional changes that our body makes. We are a race, like anything else that comes from evolution and has evolved through this: adaptation. There is no exception.

When we have two weeks under our intermittent fasting, the hormone levels control more easily. Additionally, the results manifest, which helps boost our health status when we're in this dietary approach.

It is necessary to note that fat-level control has an impact too. This effect would not only be seen by weight loss, but also indirect side benefits: enhanced heart health (less atherosclerosis or plaques of cholesterol) and better absorption of unhealthy cholesterol.

> **CHAPTER 7**

HOW TO ORGANIZE MEALS AND FASTS

There are several intermittent fasting techniques, and picking the most appropriate for your case is the first step toward success.

The 16:8 Method

The 16:8 method involves ingesting foods and calorie-containing liquids within an eight-hour window each day and fasting for the remaining 16 hours.

This is probably the most popular fasting method; it is hard to commit mistakes, if not intentionally since the schedule is clear. In addition, the 8-hour eating window can be decided in advance to adapt to your work and personal needs.

This cycle can be repeated as many times as you wish. It is highly suggested to start just once or twice per week to give your body time to adapt to this method. Then, as you gain confidence, you can attempt it for a week or more, depending on your needs.

The first thing to do to get started is pick your eight-hour window. The two most common choices are:

- 2 pm to 8 pm

- 9 am to 5 pm

If you decide to use the 12 pm–8 pm window, most of the Fasting will happen during the night, and the only real change to your lifestyle will be avoiding evening snacks and skipping breakfast.

Choosing instead the 9 am–5 pm window, you can have a rich breakfast, lunch, and a light early dinner or a late afternoon snack. However, you can experiment and pick the time frame that best fits your schedule.

This is probably the more straightforward method to follow and will help you save some money and time on cooking food each week. In addition, this method is not too stressful for the body and can be easily followed.

The biggest drawback of this and other IF methods are overeating. As already said, during the eating window, some people could start to eat more than usual, leading to weight gain and digestive problems.

I suggest beginners start with the 16:8 approach and move into more challenging methods only when their body has fully adapted to this new lifestyle. In most cases, the 16:8 approaches will already lead to excellent results.

The 14:10 Method

In some cases, starting with the 16:8 method is too

complicated, or your body does not respond as you would expect to the diet. To avoid possible side effects caused by intermittent fasting and relieve the pressure on your body, it is possible to switch to a 14:10 method.

This method is perfect for people who want to start gradually and is perfectly sustainable even for very long periods as it involves minimal changes to their lifestyle.

Unlike the 16:8 method, the eating window is longer (10 hours). This guarantees greater flexibility in managing meals and the possibility of having three meals a day without stringent time limits.

There are different eating windows that you could try; the most commons are:

- 7 am to 5 pm
- 8 am to 7 pm

There is enough time for a rich breakfast, a balanced lunch, and a light early dinner in both cases.

The 5:2 Method

The 5:2 diet is a calorie-limiting diet that follows a prescriptive program based on days of the week.

This method is particularly effective for very busy people who find it difficult to organize themselves with a fixed eating window during the week. The idea behind the 5:2 method is based on eating five days a week and substantially reducing calories consumed for the remaining two days.

5:2 can be considered a part-time diet that does not impose

strict restrictions for most of the week, allowing us to eat chocolate, pasta, or any food we desire for five days. Obviously, to avoid nullifying the chances of success of this diet, the recommendation is to consume a normal number of calories during the week and avoid falling into the phenomenon of overeating.

During the two days of calories restrictions, calorie intake should be limited to 500 calories for women and 600 for men. During the other five days, you should aim to consume around 2000 calories per day. This means that you are seeking to consume 3000 calories less or even more in an entire week. Your 500-calorie days will help regulate hunger and insulin levels, naturally reducing your appetite, making it easier to meet the 2000-calorie limit for five days of the week.

There will be no restrictions on the type of food we want to consume; the important thing is not to exceed the number of calories indicated. In terms of weight loss, following this diet strictly, a woman over 50 can expect to lose about 5 pounds per week.

This diet method is not particularly intensive for the body, and for this reason, it can also be continued for long periods or until you reach the ideal weight.

If you feel that your goals are too ambitious, you can decide to do two or more cycles to insert some breaks between them so as not to make the diet too stressful. The duration of the breaks can vary; I recommend a week so as not to lose the healthy habits you have built.

Scheduling your meals during a 5:2 diet is not strictly

required, but it might help achieve better results. I suggest keeping your meals in 12 hours, between 7 am and 7 pm, avoiding late dinners. A stricter time window can be used if you look for faster results—i.e., from 7 am. to 3 pm. By eating earlier in the day and extending the overnight fast, you will significantly help your metabolism.

For your 2000-calorie days, you have the freedom to eat whatever you like; I have added to this book some healthy recipes that can help you organize your meal plan.

During your 500-calorie days, you have to pay more attention to your diet, as it is very easy to reach and exceed 500 calories. Therefore, I suggest you focus on the following foods that usually guarantee a balanced calorie intake and allow you to create delicious recipes:

- Vegetables
- Fish
- Eggs
- Small portions of lean meat
- Soups

It is recommended to drink only water, but herbal tea and black coffee can be consumed if you want something different.

Eat-Stop-Eat Protocol

This method consists of fasting for 24 hours, twice a week, then eating "responsibly" for the other five days.

Eat-stop-eat falls in the group of methods associated with intermittent fasting dieting; unlike regular diets, calorie counting plays a secondary role in this method. Given the time restrictions, it becomes much more difficult to cheat and consume more calories than you should. Obviously, a minimum of willpower is required to respect the fasting periods and not overeat in the periods in which eating is allowed.

With eat-stop-eat, you can organize your week as you prefer; the important thing is to have two non-consecutive fasting days. This could be confusing at first, but you will always eat something on any calendar day when you adopt this method. For example, if you fast from 8 am on Tuesday to 8 am on Wednesday, you will try to have a meal just before 8 am on Tuesday and eat your next meal just after 8 am on Wednesday, fasting exactly 24 hours.

During fasting days, it is essential to maintain a high level of hydration. Therefore, especially if you decide to "eat stop eating" during hot periods, make an effort to drink frequently.

Like other intermittent fasting methods, eat-stop-eat acts on the metabolism; our body, when it is in a state of fasting for 12–36 hours, will begin to consume the glucose and then move on to burning fat.

Alternate Day Fasting

Like most intermittent fasting methods, this technique is straightforward to apply. On this diet, you fast every other day, but there are no restrictions on what you can eat on the non-fasting days.

You are free to drink as much as you want during the fasting days, but you must limit yourself only to water, unsweetened coffee, and unsweetened tea. Any other type of drink should be avoided so as not to compromise the diet. Moreover, during the fasting days, it is allowed to consume about 500 calories.

If this approach sounds similar to the 5:2 method, you are right; you can consider alternate day fasting as a more challenging version of the 5:2 method.

When and how you decide to consume your calories, the allowance does not affect the results obtained.

This method is more suitable for some people who, due to their multiple commitments, find it challenging to manage strict time constraints in their diet since you can freely decide how and when to consume the calories of the day.

We reduce calories to 500 on fasting days instead of completely zeroing them out to be able to maintain such a diet for more extended periods. Consuming zero calories could bring more significant benefits in terms of weight loss and body purification in the short term but have adverse effects on our body during a prolonged diet.

In terms of weight loss, following this method, you can expect a loss of between 3% and 8% of your body weight over a period of 2 to 12 weeks. The reason for all this variance in results lies in the boundary conditions. For example, an obese and physically active person will tend to lose much more than a slightly overweight person who does not engage in physical activity.

As I said before, you can structure your fasting days as you like in terms of calorie breakdown and what to eat during meals. In my experience, I have seen people handling better fasting days using one of the following approaches:

- One "big" meal in the late afternoon to consume all 500 calories.

- One "big" meal at lunchtime to consume all 500 calories.

- Two small meals, one around 11 am and one around 5 pm.

Alternate day fasting is perfect for losing weight for most people, but if you suffer from any congenital disease, I recommend contacting your doctor.

Spontaneous Meal Skipping

Spontaneous meal skipping is one of the easiest methods of intermittent fasting; many people do it without even realizing it. For example, do you remember when you were teenagers and skipped a meal because you woke up too late on the weekend? Spontaneous meal skipping is practically skipping a meal now and then when you get the chance.

This method is ideal, especially for beginners who are approaching intermittent fasting for the first time. My advice is to start by skipping a couple of meals a week and eventually increase to three or four. During this process, it is essential to pay attention to our body; spontaneous meal skipping is one of the IF methods with fewer side effects, but the risk of feeling tired or edgy exists. The best ways to avoid any side effects are to focus on a healthy and balanced diet and avoid skipping meals that are too close together. For example, I strongly advise against skipping two consecutive meals when using this method.

CHAPTER 8

PHYSICAL AND MENTAL
BENEFITS OBTAINED

Turning 50 opens up a whole new world of possibilities and an opportunity to discover just how we can support ourselves. Intermittent fasting is one of the answers to many questions on how to live a better, healthier life and curb or prevent diseases that develop with age.

Physical changes are bound to become more noticeable at this time, but you do not have to fear; intermittent fasting allows you to tap into your own body's resources and provide you with a solid foundation for bettering your health and overall wellness.

In this chapter, we will take a look at some of the most consequential positive effects and benefits that can be derived from intermittent fasting.

Weight Loss

Weight loss of course is the most sought-after effect of anyone on a diet, and intermittent fasting doesn't let you down. During a fast, the body goes through certain chemical reactions that induce it to start burning fat deposits rather than waiting for new calories to come in. In other words, since you are not eating, the body starts converting the fat you already have in the body into readily useable energy. Insulin levels normally increase as we ingest food, but them lower when we fast. Decreased insulin signals the body that there is a lack of incoming nutrition and that it is time to switch gears and start burning fat instead.

Another chemical reaction that takes place has to do with something called "HGH," an acronym that stands for "human growth hormone." Fasting increases these HGH levels dramatically, and it's HGH that streamlines the process of burning fat stores while also shielding us against muscle loss. Following on the heels of this recalibration, the nervous system begins delivering its special messenger of chemical change, "norepinephrine" to our fat cells. It is norepinephrine that then signals the fat to begin breaking down into what are known as "free fatty acids" that can be more easily catabolized as energy.

As you can see, due to the nature of the diet, intermittent fasting gets the body running on all metabolic cylinders. After a day of fasting, the body begins to eat away at fat stores, and then the next day, once you begin eating normally, the metabolism will pick back up where it left off, thereby allowing you to maintain the weight loss that you had achieved during your fast day. Keep this up for a long duration of time and you can lose a lot of weight. Not only that, you will lose weight in a much healthier way than would be the case in a near-starvation diet. Because once again, it is the nature of intermittent fasting that helps to shield your body from metabolic extremes, keeping you on course for targeted fat burning for the long haul.

Muscle Gain

Intermittent fasting has the potential to not only maintain muscle but to actually contribute to muscle gain. When the body goes through a period of fasting, several biological processes converge to conserve energy. As well as switching from burning incoming nutrients to burning fat deposits, the body also releases HGH (Human Growth Hormone) to conserve muscle-building proteins. HGH works overtime to make sure that during times of extra stress and strain, your muscles stay right where they are.

It's the pituitary gland that gives us HGH, and once released, this hormone only circulates for a few seconds before it is quickly used by the body. It remains somewhat misunderstood, but there is indeed a direct correlation between the production of growth hormone and the body's ability not only to maintain lean muscle but also to build it. HGH seems to help jumpstart this process.

Fasting increases the amount of HGH (Human Growth Hormone) that your body produces. Heavy consumption of carbs, on the other hand, significantly reduces it. Therefore, through the process of intermittent fasting, you can get your HGH back up and running and even gain a little muscle in the process. It is precisely for this reason that some athletes actually take shots of HGH to improve their muscle production. But we don't have to buy an expensive shot of HGH from the doctor; we can simply produce our own from regular rounds of intermittent fasting.

Improved Fertility

It's true, that intermittent fasting could indeed improve fertility rates among women. The human body you see has a natural—built-in—capability when it comes to allowing or hindering a woman's ability to get pregnant. This is why near-starvation diets are bad. These kinds of drastic changes in food intake make the body think that it is starving, and a time of famine is simply not a good time to get pregnant!

But having that said, intermittent fasting allows for the body to slim down and burn some fat while still keeping everything on an even enough keel to promote fertility. Intermittent fasting can even improve fertility levels by recalibrating the body's system during the fast/eat cycles. Even more intriguing, recent studies have shown that women who are dealing with complications from Polycystic Ovarian Syndrome (or as it are otherwise known "PCOS") can have their symptoms greatly reduced by engaging in regular intermittent fasting.

For women with PCOS, the periodic reduction in calories actually helps to fortify special "luteinizing hormones" that are crucial in regulating ovulation. In other words—it makes women more fertile, by having them produce eggs at more regular intervals. Intermittent fasting as it turns out is great at rebooting the system in a wide variety of ways and improved fertility is just another benefit gleaned from the overall results. This dietary approach makes for more streamlined ovulation. And the resulting improvement in fertility thereof is just another proof of this wonderful recalibration process at work.

Reduced Inflammation

Inflammation is a natural reaction of the body's immune system when things are just a little bit unbalanced. For example, if you happen to skin your knee, inflammation develops on the site of the injury to keep the wound from bleeding excessively and to clear out toxins. The resulting scab that a skinned knee produces is a function of inflammation. Without the production of a scabby inflamed tissue, the wound would continue to bleed. In this situation, inflammation is obviously a good thing.

It is indeed a crucial function of our body, and it most certainly serves a purpose. But too much inflammation when it is not warranted can become a problem rather than a solution. Intermittent fasting can help clear up this chronic inflammation. It achieves this through the creation of something called "beta-hydroxybutyrate"—a natural beta-blocker that decreases the immune response when it comes to inflammation. This is good news for those that suffer from ailments such as arthritis and the like.

During intermittent fasting, beta-hydroxybutyrate is released and immediately begins to work blocking certain receptors of the immune system that are responsible for inflammation. And it's the powerful immune receptor, the so-called "NLRP3 inflammasome" in particular that beta-hydroxybutyrate immediately latches onto and subdues its inflammatory response.

Again, inflammation is a natural response of the body and

in some cases is necessary. However, chronic inflammation leads to such things as arthritis and hypertension. In today's world, much of the food we eat is overly processed and loaded with carbohydrates. This, my friends, is simply a recipe for unwarranted and out-of-control inflammation. However, intermittent fasting allows the body to scale back this process and reduce unnecessary inflammation.

Body Detox

Intermittent fasting puts the body through a process called "autophagy." The term literally means "self-eating." As strange as it might sound, it's a very beneficial process in which the body seeks out damaged or dead cellular material, consumes this excess junk, and then spits it back out as brand new healthy cells. In other words, it's a process by which we can detox.

Autophagy is a routine process that occurs all the time, but typically at a much slower rate than it does during periods of fasting. However, intermittent fasting kicks autophagy into high gear and allows your body to detox itself of toxins, waste, and dead cellular debris—you name it, at a much faster pace. It shifts the body from burning carbs to burning fat, and in doing so, it also automatically kick-starts the process of autophagy.

You may now be noticing a theme in this book, which seems to touch upon every aspect of intermittent fasting. Fasting at its core is a practice that sends the body into a kind of standby mode in which vital processes are kept running by conserving and making use of material that is already available. For us humans, that material is our stored fat, as well as cellular debris.

By using fasting to get ourselves into this stasis state, we reap the benefit of burning up fat stores as well as detoxing our system of needless cellular waste. Like a clean-up crew suddenly summoned to aisle 2—autophagy mops up the mess and gets the ball rolling. If you really want to detox, put down that fruit juice and pick up intermittent fasting instead!

Reduced Stress/Hypertension

A steady regimen of intermittent fasting could very well lower your blood pressure. In fact, a recent study that appeared in an edition of "Nutrition and Healthy Aging" back in 2018 noted that among 23 test subjects, those who engaged in a regular intermittent fast experienced a significant drop in blood pressure.

A leading cause of hypertension is an overabundance of inflammation in the body. And as mentioned, intermittent fasting helps to reduce that inflammation. In addition to this, intermittent fasting has also shown itself to be a direct factor in the reduction of stress and hypertension. An intermittent fast lowers insulin levels, and with it, both symptoms of hypertension and stress are considerably eased.

Most probably think of stress as "mental stress," but in reality, our bodies face stress all the time on a holistic level through what is termed "oxidative stress." And more often than not, this biological oxidative stress, when in overabundance, can lead to psychological stress. Many patients suffering from anxiety, depression, and the like have been found to have inordinately high levels of oxidative stress in their cellular makeup. Intermittent fasting helps to shield our body's cells from undergoing too much oxidative stress by reducing the incidence of harmful molecules called free radicals in the body.

Free radicals are molecules that are highly unstable and contain "highly reactive electrons." It's these free radicals that bounce around the body bumping into other molecules and disrupting their own charge. This in turn creates a domino effect in which the disrupted molecules themselves become free radicals and as the collateral damage adds up, it leads to tremendous oxidative stress on the cells of the body. Free radicals often originate from faulty mitochondria within our cells.

It is the detoxifying state of autophagy that cleans the house and gets rid of such faulty cellular material, thereby preventing the rise of free radicals. This in turn reduces oxidative stress. Oxidative stress is no joke and can cause a wide variety of problems. But autophagy gets right to the root of the problem; this then reduces stress and hypertension as a whole—all across the board.

Lower Cholesterol Levels

While more research still needs to be done—studies have indeed shown that regular intermittent fasting has the propensity to lower that "bad cholesterol" known as LDL, which stands for "low-density lipoproteins." These lipoproteins are responsible for bringing our cholesterol levels to unhealthy heights, but intermittent fasting can greatly reduce their prevalence. In fact, recent research has indicated that study participants who engaged in intermittent fasting for roughly 3 months, managed to cut down their LDL by as much as 25 percent.

There has been some argument in recent years over whether or not those who have high cholesterol should engage in intermittent fasting. And to be sure, if you have high cholesterol, be sure to consult your doctor before starting this fasting regimen. But as these recent studies have shown, if done properly, long-term intermittent fasting could indeed have the capacity to significantly lower cholesterol levels.

Increased Longevity

Did we mention that intermittent fasting can help you live longer? Yes, if nothing else, it might actually help you live longer! There have been many studies recently that have shown the benefits of caloric restrictions. For example, mice that have been subjected to an intermittent fast have been shown to actually live longer.

So, if you think that eating those microwaveable hot pockets every lunch break is killing you, you just might be onto something! Because our heavily processed foods loaded with carbohydrates are not only making us fatter, but also increasing the disruption posed by free radicals, creating oxidative stress, and producing unbearable inflammation. Intermittent fasting could be a cure for all of these things and, as a result, could very well increase your longevity. As you can see, there are more than enough reasons to give intermittent fasting a try. So, what are you waiting for?

CHAPTER 9
HOW TO OVERCOME OBSTACLES

This chapter will delve into the possible negative side effects of fasting intermittently. Some people who swear by this practice may not be willing to admit that there are unpleasant side effects of fasting intermittently. But that would be myopic and withholding vital information.

Having said that, it is important to point out that the general downsides of intermittent fasting are common to all women regardless of age. While women of childbearing age might have effects on their reproductive hormones, post-menopausal women or older women may not need to worry about reproduction, although they experience frequent changes in their moods, difficulty in sleeping, and occasional headaches.

After a comprehensive review of several scientific studies on women's health, fasting, and aging, researchers weren't able to find any significant negative effect of intermittent fasting and point to a lack of research on the topic (Journal of Mid-Life Health, 2016). These types of scientific reviews are very useful for getting unbiased information that gives you a broader picture of several results from different related studies performed over many years. Comprehensive reviews cut down prejudices often associated with smaller studies that may have been sponsored by special interest groups. Overall, scientific studies show encouraging results in different aspects of women's health including mental health, physical health, and weight loss. That is not to say there are no negative side effects of this regimen. It only means that the negative side effects of intermittent fasting are common to women of all ages—both pre and post-menopausal women and depend largely on the individual woman.

With that being said, not everyone who practices intermittent fasting will have a negative side effect. These differ from person to person. The important thing is being aware of these negative side effects and learning how to handle them if they occur. Also, remember that most of the off-putting effects of fasting intermittently don't last beyond the first few days. Within a week or two, your body would have adjusted to your new eating schedule and any negative effects will gradually subside until things feel back to normal. So it is important to allow your body some time to adjust instead of trying it for one or two days and throwing in the towel.

Here is how to deal with some of the common negative side affects you will likely encounter as you start your new eating habits.

Hunger

One of the first not-so-fun and most obvious results of fasting is hunger. This side effect is difficult because going without food longer than your body is conditioned to will result in an uncomfortable desire for anything to eat. All your life, you have programmed your body to expect food at certain times throughout the day. It would be weird if you suddenly change your eating pattern, and your body accepts the change without putting up at least a little resistance. If your body doesn't get food at the time it normally does, a hormone called ghrelin—the hunger hormone—will start acting up to remind you that you should supply your body with food. This "acting up" or reminder to eat at your usual time will continue until your brain convinces ghrelin to accept your new eating schedule. But until then, you will likely feel intense hunger, but don't worry, it will pass. You will need to tap into your reserve of mental strength to stay committed to your course.

To effectively handle hunger pangs, drink more water, or any qualifying beverage when fasting. Doing so will help to suppress hunger pangs. Quite often, the feeling of hunger is not necessarily an indication that you are hungry; it might be a slight dip in your blood sugar level—something that water or other non-calorie liquids can take care of.

To help delay hunger on your fasting days or during the fasting window (depending on the type of fasting regimen you choose to follow), ensure that you include adequate amounts of healthy fats, carbs, and proteins in your meals before commencing your fast. Also, during your fast, try to keep your mind off food. Combining low-impact exercises with fasting can help give you the boost you need to go through your day without feeling too uncomfortable. Getting enough sleep will also help you throughout the day; there is nothing that will upset your day more than lack of sleep at night and having to fast. That is an open invitation for fatigue and hunger!

Frequent Urination

As with hunger, it is also expected to experience an increase in the number of times you urinate. There is no mystery here as intermittent fasting requires that you increase your intake of water and other liquids to stay hydrated. This will in turn increase the frequency of urination. Keep drinking your water and don't avoid bathroom visits. Holding it for too long can weaken your bladder muscles and trying not to drink water will soon make you dehydrated and provide the next side effect—both bad!

Headaches

Intermittent fasting can make your blood sugar take a nosedive. This introduces stress on your body, your brain will release stress hormones, and you will likely experience some degree of headache. Dehydration can lead to headaches during fasting as your body is telling you it lacks adequate water.

To reduce the occurrence of headaches, try to minimize

stress on your body. It is okay to exercise during fasting, but excessive exercise can trigger a large amount of stress. Also, try to keep your body hydrated at all times by drinking enough water. But don't chug water in a rush and don't drink water excessively. Too much water can result in an imbalance in your mineral and body water ratio.

Cravings

It is normal to experience more than usual cravings for food during your fasting window. This is a biological and psychological response to the feeling of deprivation that is often associated with going without food. And because your body is all out to get glucose, you might notice that you crave more sugar or carbohydrates. These cravings don't mean that you are less committed to your goals. Rather, cravings happen to remind you that you are human. Even ardent practitioners of intermittent fasting experience cravings from time to time.

When you start craving something, remind yourself of your goal and distract yourself from food-related topics. Keep your mind engrossed with other non-food-related activities such as hobbies, taking a walk in nature, or going to sleep for a while. During your eating window, you can treat yourself to a healthy bite of what you crave to minimize the intensity of the craving or longing. Remind yourself during your fasting window that you will soon eat what you long for, so there's no need to dwell on it or give it too much thought when it is not yet time to eat. Remind your body that you are no longer a teenager or a young adult. You have had lots of experience in curbing your cravings, and this case is not an exception.

Heartburn, Bloating, and Constipation

Occasionally, heartburn can occur when your stomach produces acids for the digestion of your food, but there is no food present in the stomach to be digested. Bloating and constipation usually go hand in hand and can also occur in some cases. Together, these two can make you feel very uncomfortable.

Drinking adequate amounts of water can reduce the risk of heartburn, bloating, and constipation. Heartburns can also be minimized by cutting down on spicy foods during your eating window. If you experience heartburn during intermittent fasting, here's something you can try before going to sleep. Prop yourself up when you lie down to sleep. But don't use pillows to prop yourself as that will put more pressure on your stomach and increase the discomfort. Use a specially designed wedge or use a 6-inch block or something similar to elevate your head as you lie down. Doing this will make gravity minimize the backward flow of your stomach contents into your gullet. Propping yourself this way should bring you relief from heartburn. However, if heartburn, bloating, and constipation persist, consult your doctor immediately.

Binging

Eating a large amount as soon as the fasting window is

over is usually associated with first-timers fasting. The intense hunger of fasting can drive you to eat in a hurry when breaking and you can end up overeating. In some cases, binging can be a result of a simple misunderstanding of the basics of intermittent fasting. They assume that they can eat as much as they want in the eating window since the no-eating window will take care of calories. This misunderstanding can deprive you of gaining any significant benefits that come with fasting intermittently, especially if you are looking to shed some weight. Binging or overeating in your eating window will reverse all the hard work you put in during the fast.

To avoid binging, be sure to plan the size and type of meal well ahead of the eating window. Don't start fasting without knowing what portion you are going to consume at the end. Waiting until you can eat to decide what to eat and how much to eat can lead to overeating because your food choices will be largely influenced by how hungry you feel.

Low Energy

Feeling exhausted is a normal part of fasting. Until your body gets used to sourcing its fuel from fat storage, you are likely to experience some decline in your energy levels. Usually, they get back up within a couple of days.

To help stay energized, tailor your activities to remain low-key, at least at first. There is no need to push yourself to prove that you are a strong woman. Deciding to practice intermittent fasting is enough proof that you are mentally, emotionally, and physically strong. Since you are not in competition with anyone, it is in your best interest to conserve energy as much as possible. Get a massage, spend time relaxing in bed, or sleep if you have to. These little activities can go a long way in keeping you energized.

Feeling Cold

Some people experience an extra feeling of cold during fasting. If you experience this, there is no cause for alarm. It might be the result of a drop in your blood sugar level. Usually, blood flow to your internal fat storage is increased during fasting. As a result of this increase, your fat is moved to parts of your body where it needs to be used as energy. This can make other parts of your body that have less fat storage experience cold. So if you feel cold in your fingers or toes, it is your body doing its fat-burning process for your own good.

To help reduce the cold, put on layers, stay in warm places, drink hot coffee or tea (with no calories), or take a hot shower. It is important to keep in mind that feeling cold is just a result of fasting and does not mean you are ill. So avoid the urge to self-medicate. If the cold feeling persists even on your non-fasting days or during your eating window, consult your doctor.

Mood Swing

Imagine the following combinations. Stress on your body

is caused by the dip in your blood sugar. Your hormones are going berserk from the various reactions going on in your body as a result of not eating normally, or on schedule. The lethargic feeling from lack of food, hunger, and cravings constantly telling you to eat. Not being able to socialize with others freely because of your new eating pattern, you can't wine and dine at social events if it is outside your eating window! All of these can lead to a psychological state of feeling annoyed or irritated.

The surest way to minimize mood swings resulting from intermittent fasting is to deliberately keep your attention off issues that set you on edge and focus on what you are doing and what makes you happy. The more you keep your mind wrapped up in gratitude and appreciation, the better you will feel. So, during your fasting window, be deliberate about engaging in things that lift your spirits and keep your mind on happy and productive thoughts.

Bottom Line

Intermittent fasting is a lifestyle regimen that is safe for older practitioners. It is a medical intervention that can bring about improvements in many aspects of a woman's health. However, it is not suitable for every person. If you notice that you have severe negative reactions to intermittent fasting, it is in your best interest to desist at once and consult your doctor. No rule makes it compulsory to complete a fast once you begin. You can absolutely break in the middle of your fasting window (even if it is just that day) if you can no longer endure unpleasant side effects and try again at a later time.

While it is okay to give your body a few weeks to get used to your new eating pattern, it is also crucial to pay close attention to what your body is telling you. Thankfully, as an older woman with experience, you can tell when something works for you or not. You know when you can commit to something and when you can't find the motivation to follow through. I believe that, as a woman with a tremendous wealth of experience, you will find the strength to stick to your resolve within reason.

CHAPTER 10
EXTRA

The 5 Best Teas & the 5 Best Infusions for Intermittent Fasting and Weight Loss

Teas

    1. **Green Tea**

Green Tea is the most famous and generally smashed tea, with health advantages. Drinking Green Tea diminishes mortality and forestalls cardiovascular illness. This tea, what's more, has been found to consume fat stores in the body. This cycle has been consummated by extricating the Green Tea concentrate and making it into a pill form.

Green Tea was seasoned by the Asians and isn't aged, but it dries and delivers a green leaf. It is lighter and the tannins are the synthetic substances in green tea, which tie surface proteins in our mouths to create a fixing result debilitating plaque-shaping microorganisms. It supports the processing of slick substances and is remembered to standardize digestion. It likewise contains a characteristic fluoride, which forestalls tooth rot. Scientists feel this resembles a sterile effect.

2. Black Tea

Black tea, frequently alluded to as the "recuperating tea," has numerous mental advantages, with few actual ones. Black tea is the most run-of-the-mill among all tea-drinking races. In contrast to the degrees of caffeine in espresso or its cousin green tea, dark tea has lower measures of caffeine, which elevates blood flow to the cerebrum. This tea essentially expands fixation and memory, contains minor component fluoride forestalling tooth rot, and mitigating synthetics to assist with digestion.

Black tea's helpful impacts on gastrointestinal and gastric diseases are a direct result of its tannins. They discharge tannins from dark tea leaves when soaks for a total of 15 minutes, they decline digestive brokenness and are amazing antidiarrheal. Black Tea opens the flow in vessels and keeps up with the solid circulatory strain. To wrap things up, black tea's theophylline works on the degrees of good cholesterol.

3. Oolong Tea

Oolong tea is a mix of dark tea and green tea. The genuine brand names of oolong tea might contain upwards of 20 unique sorts of tea. Oolong tea is genuinely extraordinary in mix and flavor. At this phase of tea drinking, one should buy a more extreme tea, which is generally little, oval in shape, and holds the tea leaves in when you place it in a cup, this is the method involved with soaking the tea. Eliminate when the dim shading appears.

4. White Tea

Made by utilizing youthful tea leaves that stay shrouded in down, white tea leaves aren't aged. All things being equal, they are steamed and dried in the sun. On account of having less aging, white tea contains a higher centralization of synthetic mixtures known to assist with battling disease. The fermented tea has a shiny white appearance due to the wool leaves. It has a pleasant fragrance and new flavor.

5. Ginseng Tea

Ginseng tea is one of the world's most famous teas. It comes from the ginseng root. Its mending properties have deductively been demonstrated to come from a lot of regular synthetic substances known as ginsenosides, which are a strong adaptogen. We can make this tea from the leaves of the plant, which resembles different teas like the green and oolong assortments. Nonetheless, this is neither as famous nor as significant as a tea arranged from the roots principally because the helpful ginsenosides are inside the meaty servings of the plant.

The interaction applied to the ginseng root decides its shade of one or the other red or white ginseng tea. Red ginseng comes from the unpeeled attaches being exposed to regular steaming, which becomes them into a rosy earthy colored tint, after which they dry. White ginseng is produced using stripped ginseng roots, which are then quickly dried under sunlight.

Infusions

6. Elderflower Infusion

Ingredients:

- 2 teaspoons elderberry flowers

Put to heat the water and once it is hot, insert your sachet and leave for 5 minutes. Drink when it is still hot. Excellent for those who are influenced. Your herbal tea is ready.

7. Marigold and Lemon Balm Infusion

Ingredients:

- 2 tablespoons calendula flowers

- 10 lemon balm leaves

- 1 lime

To prepare the calendula and lemon balm infusion, bring 2 liters of water to a boil. Dip the marigold flowers and put out the fire. Leave to infuse for 10 minutes. Filter the drink and pour it into a glass bottle. Leave to cool to room temperature. Add the well-washed and dried lemon balm leaves, and add the sliced lime. Transfer to the fridge and serve cold.

8. Infusion of Garlic and Lemon

Ingredients:

- 1 garlic

- 1 lemon

Wash the lemon, preferably with a thick peel, and put it whole in a small saucepan, so that the amount of water can cover it. Then, add the garlic clove. Bring to a boil and let it boil for 7 minutes, no more. Do not raise the flame too much, and do not extend the boiling time. Remove the saucepan from the heat, remove the lemon and the garlic clove and let it cool.

9. Infusion of Olive Leaves

Ingredients:

- 5 g dried olive leaves

Boil the leaves in water for a few minutes, let stand and cool, then filter and drink. The generally recommended dose is one cup per day.

10.   Sage Infusion

Ingredients:

- 5 leaves of dried sage

- A few drops lemon juice

- 1 teaspoon honey (optional)

Bring the water to a boil and leave the dried sage leaves to infuse for about 10 minutes, filter and add a few drops of lemon juice, and, if you wish, a teaspoon of honey. Let it cool down and drink.

Exercises

Squat to Chair

Seat squats are a beginner-friendly exercise extraordinary for building significant leg muscles like your quads, hamstrings, and gluteus while offering the help of a firm surface.

1. Stand tall with your feet hip-width apart. Your hips, knees, and toes should make all points forward. (Hold free weights in your hands to make it harder.)

2. Curve your knees and expand your bum backward as though you will sit once again onto a seat. Ensure that you keep your knees behind your toes and your weight on your heels. Stand back up and repeat.

Forearm Plank

Although it's a challenge to do it correctly, the Forearm Plank fortifies the abs, legs, and core once you get the hang of it. It is also helpful in extending your feet' curves just as your calves, shoulders, and hamstrings.

1. On the floor with your lower arms level, ensuring that your elbows are adjusted straightforwardly under your shoulders.

2. Draw in your center and raise your body off the floor, keeping your lower arms on the floor and your body in an orderly fashion from head to feet. Keep your abs drawn in and do whatever it takes not to allow your hips to rise or drop. Rather than 8 to 12 reps, hold for 30 seconds. If it hurts your lower back or turns out to be excessively troublesome, place your knees down on the ground.

Modified Push-Up

If you have trouble doing regular push-ups effectively, you can always switch to modified push-ups. It works on your upper body.

1. Start in a bowing situation on a tangle with hands beneath shoulders and knees behind hips, so the back is calculated and long.

2. Fold toes under, fix abs, and twist elbows to bring down the chest toward the floor. Keep your view before your fingertips, so your neck remains long.

3. Press chest rears up to the beginning position.

Bird Dog

It is a simple exercise that improves stability and reduces lower back pain. It also helps to maintain proper posture.

1. Kneel on the ground on all fours.

2. Stand at one arm long, draw in the abs, and stretch the opposite leg long behind you.

3. Repeat 8 to multiple times and then switch sides.

Shoulder Overhead Press

1. Start with feet hip-width apart. Bring elbows out to the side, making a goal-line position with arms, hand weights along the edge of the head, and abs tight.

2. Press free weights gradually up until arms are straight. Slowly return to the initial point. Whenever wanted, you can likewise do this activity situated in a seat.

Chest Fly

1. Hold a couple of hand weights carefully shrouded and place your shoulder bones and head on top of the ball with the remainder of your body in a tabletop position.

2. The feet ought to be hip-width apart. Raise free weights together straight over the chest, palms looking in. Gradually lower your arms out to the side with a slight twist in your elbow until your elbows are about chest level.

Standing Calf Raise

1. Remain on the edge of a stage.

2. Or then again, if you have a stage heart stimulating exercise stage; place two arrangements of risers under the stage.

3. Stand tall with your abs pulled in, the soles of your feet solidly planted on the progression, and your impact points looming over the edge.

4. Lean your hands against a wall or a solid object for balance.

5. Raise your heels a couple of crawls over the edge of the progression, so you're on your tiptoes.

6. Hold the situation briefly, and afterward, bring down your heels beneath the stage, feeling a stretch

in your lower leg muscles.

Single-Leg Hamstring Bridge

1. Lie on your back with twisted knees hip-width apart, and feet level.

2. Crush gluteus and lift hips off the tangle into a scaffold. Lower and lift the hips for 8–12 reps, then repeat on the opposite side.

Bent-Over Row

The composition is exceptionally significant with the twisted around the column, and the ideal approach to guarantee you don't get messy is to pick the perfect measure of weight. Slow, controlled developments are more incentive than snapping up an enormous weight and contorting everywhere in the shop.

1. When you have your hand weight stacked, remain with your feet shoulder-width apart. Twist your knees and lean forward from the midsection.

2. Your knees ought to be twisted. However, your back stays straight, with your neck by your spine. Get the bar with your hands (palms-down), only more extensive than shoulder-width apart, and let it hang

with your arms straight.

3. Support your center and crush your shoulders together to push the load up until it contacts your sternum. At that point, gradually drop it back down once more. There's one rep. With a lightweight, go for 4 sets of 8 to 10 reps.

Basic Abs

The best abs exercises are ones that work something other than one part of your muscular strength. Indeed, there are various layers of muscles (in addition to delicate tissue, nerves, and veins) that make up the entire stomach wall. Also, even though you can't see or truly feel them all, they're genuinely significant for keeping your whole body solid and stable.

There are various types of abs exercises. Here are two of them to keep it simple for you.

Abdominal Hold

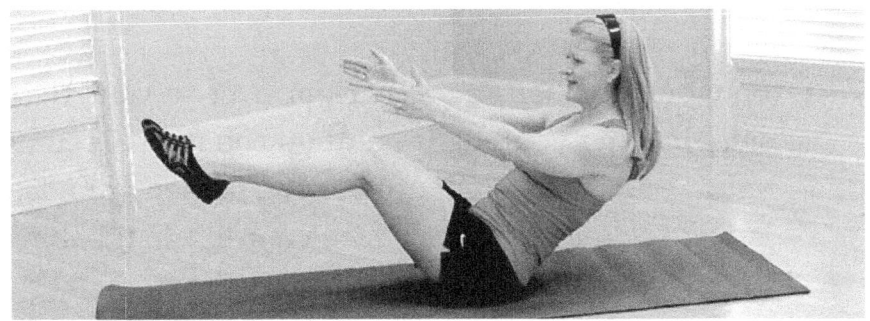

1. Sit tall on the edge of a solid seat (or step with four risers) and spot your hands on the border with your

fingers highlighting your knees.

2. Fix your abs and carry your toes 2 to 4 inches off the floor. Lift your butt off the seat.

3. Hold this situation; however long you can—focus on 5 to 10 seconds. Let yourself down and repeat. Proceed for 1 minute.

The Side Crunch

1. Bow on the floor and lean right over to your right side, putting your right palm on the floor. Keeping your weight-adjusted, gradually broaden your left leg and point your toes. Place your left hand above your head, guiding your elbow to the roof.

2. Then, gradually lift your leg to hip height as you expand your arm over your leg, with your palm looking forward. Put your hand over while bringing

the left half of your ribs to stay near your hip.

3. Lower to your beginning position and repeat 6 to multiple times. Complete 2 sets of 6 to 8 reps, and afterward switch sides.

QUICK RECIPES

BREAKFAST RECIPES

EGGS AND SALSA

NUTRINION

- Calories: 383
- Fat: 14 g
- Fiber: 4 g
- Carbohydrates: 3 g
- Protein: 8 g

PREPARATION TIME **5 MIN**   COOKING TIME **5 MIN**   SERVINGS **2**

INGREDIENTS

- 3 cups tomatoes
- 1 green onion (bunch)
- 1 bunch cilantro, chopped
- 1 cup red onion, chopped
- Juice from 1 lime
- 2 small habanero chilies, chopped
- 2 garlic cloves, minced
- 8 eggs, whisked
- A drizzle olive oil
- A pinch sea salt

DIRECTIONS

1. Mix tomatoes, green onions, red onion, habaneros, garlic, cilantro, and lime juice and toss well.

2. Add a pinch of salt, toss again and keep this in the fridge until you serve it.

3. Heat up a pan with a drizzle of oil, add eggs, and scramble them for 4 to 5 minutes.

4. Divide scrambled eggs between plates, add salsa on top, and serve.

POACHED EGG

NUTRINION

- Calories: 200
- Fat: 8 g
- Fiber: 2 g
- Carbohydrates: 8 g
- Protein: 6 g

PREPARATION TIME **5 MIN**   COOKING TIME **5 MIN**   SERVINGS **3**

INGREDIENTS

- 1 tbsp rice vinegar
- 1 egg
- Salt to taste
- Black pepper to taste
- Water to fill pot

DIRECTIONS

1. Put some water into a pot and heat up.

2. Simmer gently, add vinegar and whisk.

3. Crack the egg into simmering water and cook for 4 minutes making sure it stays in a compact shape.

4. Transfer the egg to a plate and serve with salt and pepper for breakfast.

CREAMY RASPBERRY CHEESECAKE BITES

NUTRINION

PREPARATION TIME **10 MIN**   COOKING TIME **30 MIN**   SERVINGS **4**

INGREDIENTS

- ¾ cup butter

- 6 drops liquid stevia

- 2 tsp pure vanilla

- 1/8 tsp plus a pinch of sea salt, divided

- ¾ cup raw unsalted cashews

- ¼ cup fresh raspberries, halved (frozen berries work, just thaw and drain them well)

- ¼ cup raw unsalted pecans

- 1/8 tsp ground cinnamon

DIRECTIONS

1. Place the butter, stevia, vanilla, and 1/8 teaspoon of salt and blend. Pulse until the mixture is smooth. Scrape down the sides.

2. Add the cashews and process until nuts are broken down to the size of aquarium gravel or smaller.

3. Add the raspberries to a bowl. Stir them by hand and don't worry if some of them break while others stay whole. Cover and refrigerate for 30 minutes. The mixture will become firm.

4. Grind the pecans into a near flour-like state. Add cinnamon and salt.

5. Remove the batter from the refrigerator. Scoop out a tablespoon of the cheesecake mixture with a melon baller. While the batter is still in the melon baller, press the open end into the pecan dust. This is the flat side.

6. Release the batter with the flat side down on a plate. You have just made a cheesecake bite.

7. Before serving, put it in the refrigerator for about an hour.

DECADENT CHERRY CHOCOLATE ALMOND CLUSTERS

NUTRINION

- Calories: 260
- Fat: 25 g
- Fiber: 2 g
- Carbohydrates: 8 g
- Protein: 2 g

PREPARATION TIME **10 MIN**   COOKING TIME **25 MIN**   SERVINGS **5**

INGREDIENTS

- 1 tbsp smooth nut butter of your choice
- 8 oz. dark chocolate
- 1 cup oats
- 1/3 cup raw unsalted nuts, chopped
- 1/3 cup dried, unsweetened cherries or raisins, chopped
- 1 cup Water

DIRECTIONS

1. Boil water and simmer and then add the nut butter and chocolate, stirring occasionally for 2 to 3 minutes.

2. Take out from heat and stir in the oats, nuts, and dried fruit.

3. Stripe a baking sheet with wax or parchment paper.

4. Drib the batter with a rounded teaspoonful onto the baking sheet, making 20 mounds.

5. Leave the baking sheet in the refrigerator for 25 minutes or until the mounds are set. Remove and store in an airtight container.

LOW-CARB WAFFLES

NUTRINION

- Calories: 200
- Fat: 8 g
- Fiber: 2 g
- Carbohydrates: 8 g
- Protein: 6 g

PREPARATION TIME **10 MIN**   COOKING TIME **20 MIN**   SERVINGS **4**

INGREDIENTS

- 6 eggs
- 2 mashed bananas
- 2 tsp unsweetened almond butter
- 3 tsp quinoa flour
- ¼ tsp salt
- ½ tsp cinnamon powder
- ½ tsp extra-virgin olive oil
- ½ tbsp coconut butter
- ½ tbsp almond butter
- ¼ banana, sliced
- ¼ tbsp walnuts chopped
- 1 tbsp maple syrup

DIRECTIONS

1. Plug in the waffle maker and let it heat up.

2. Get a mixing container and mix in it the mashed bananas, eggs, quinoa flour, cinnamon, unsweetened almond butter, and salt until you get a smooth mixture.

3. When the waffle maker is hot enough, use the extra-virgin olive oil to grease it.

4. Divide the waffle mixture into three portions and cook each until it is ready. Remove and do the same for the remaining mixture as well.

5. When cooled off, top the waffles with the remaining almond butter, quarter sliced bananas, chopped walnuts, maple syrup, and coconut butter.

BACON TACOS

NUTRINION

- Calories: 260
- Fat: 8 g
- Fiber: 2 g
- Carbohydrates: 8 g
- Protein: 45 g

PREPARATION TIME 10 MIN   COOKING TIME 20 MIN   SERVINGS 4

INGREDIENTS

- 14 pieces halved bacon
- 1 avocado, seeded, peeled, and sliced
- ¼ tsp black pepper powder
- ½ cup Monterey jack shredded
- 5 eggs
- 2 tbsp fresh chives chopped
- 1 tbsp almond milk
- A pinch salt
- 1 tbsp unsweetened butter
- A little hot sauce

DIRECTIONS

1. Begin by preparing the taco shells first.

2. Heat the oven in advance at 400°F.

3. Get a baking sheet and line the inside with foil. Place the bacon strips in it, crisscrossing each other to form a square at the end. Do this again to form three consecutive weaves.

4. Take the black pepper powder and season the arranged bacon pieces and press flat the bacon using a baking rack that is inverted.

5. Place the sheet for baking in the oven that you heated in advance and let the bacon bake until it is crispy, which will take half an hour.

6. When the bacon is ready, using a knife for paring, cut up the crispy bacon squares to form small circles, which will be the taco shells. This should be done very fast.

7. Get the eggs and crack them in a mixing container. Add the almond milk and whisk both until they are well mixed.

8. Take a frying pan and over medium heat melt the unsweetened butter.

9. Follow this by pouring the whisked egg mixture and slowly moving the eggs around to turn them into scrambled eggs. Add salt and black pepper powder for seasoning followed by chives then remove the frying pan from the heat.

10. Get a plate that you will use to serve and arrange the bacon taco shells on top of it.

11. Add the scrambled eggs on top of the bacon taco shells, and then add a little cheese, avocado slices, and a little hot sauce as well.

DELICIOUS SHAKSHUKA

NUTRINION

- Calories: 40
- Fat: 1 g
- Fiber: 2 g
- Carbohydrates: 8 g
- Protein: 2 g

PREPARATION TIME 10 MIN   **COOKING TIME 30 MIN**   **SERVINGS 4**

INGREDIENTS

- ¼ cup feta cheese, crumbled
- 2 tbsp extra-virgin olive oil
- 8 eggs
- 1 onion, sliced
- 1 tsp black pepper powder
- 2 Red bell peppers, sliced
- ¼ tsp salt
- 3 minced garlic cloves
- ½ tsp red pepper flakes
- 3 tomatoes, blended
- ½ tsp coriander
- 2 tsp cumin powder
- 1 tsp paprika
- 1 tsp fresh parsley chopped
- Pieces of almond bread

DIRECTIONS

1. Heat your oven in advance at 375°F.

2. Heat the olive oil in a large frying pan over medium heat.

3. Add the sliced onion and let it fry until it is a nice golden color. Top it off with the red bell pepper pieces and let this cook until the bell peppers are soft.

4. Add the minced garlic cloves to this mixture as well and let it cook until the garlic is nice and fragrant.

5. Add the sliced tomato, cumin powder, coriander, paprika, and red pepper flakes. Also, add the salt and black pepper powder. Let this mix cook for 10 minutes until it thickens.

6. Get a large baking tin and pour in the cooked sauce. Using a spoon, create eight holes in the sauce and crack an egg in each and pour it in.

7. Sprinkle a little salt and pepper over the eggs for seasoning. Using aluminum foil, cover the baking tin and transfer it into the oven you heated in advance for 15 minutes until the eggs are well cooked.

8. When they are ready, sprinkle the feta cheese that has been crumbled on top together with the fresh parsley as well.

9. Cut out slices and serve with the almond bread.

EGGS WITH CAULIFLOWER

NUTRINION

- Calories: 40
- Fat: 1 g
- Fiber: 2 g
- Carbohydrates: 8 g
- Protein: 2 g

PREPARATION TIME **10 MIN**   COOKING TIME **20 MIN**   SERVINGS **4**

INGREDIENTS

- ½ cauliflower head
- 1 tbsp extra-virgin olive oil
- 3 eggs
- ¼ tsp black pepper freshly ground
- ¼ tsp salt
- ¼ tsp cornstarch
- 1 cup cheddar cheese shredded
- 2 bacon slices
- 2 tsp paprika
- 1 tsp fresh chives
- 1 small pot of Boiling water

DIRECTIONS

1. Get a box grater, and with it, grate the half head of cauliflower until it is well grated.

2. Place the grated cauliflower into a mixing container and add an egg to it together with the shredded cheddar cheese, cornstarch, pepper, and salt. Mix them all well.

3. Get a large frying pan and heat the olive oil over medium heat. Using a serving spoon, scoop the cauliflower mix into the frying pan and shape it into patties.

4. Cook these patties for 5 minutes until they are crispy and done. Ensure to flip both sides.

5. Get a saucepan and poach the remaining 2 eggs over medium heat using boiling water.

6. Get another pan for frying and over a medium flame, let the olive oil become hot. Follow this by adding bacon pieces and allowing them to cook until they are crispy.

7. Crack the eggs and remove them from the shell. Slice them into circles.

8. Place the cooked cauliflower patties on a plate and add the sliced eggs together with the slices of crispy bacon. Sprinkle the paprika and chives and serve.

NUTRINION

- Calories: 100
- Fat: 7 g
- Fiber: 2 g
- Carbohydrates: 8 g
- Protein: 6 g

PREPARATION TIME **20MIN**   COOKING TIME **25 MIN**   SERVINGS **4**

INGREDIENTS

- 6 large eggs
- 1 cup trimmed and halved Brussels sprouts
- ¼ tsp black pepper, freshly ground
- 6 bacon slices
- ¼ tsp salt
- 2 tbsp extra-virgin olive oil
- 3 tbsp buffalo sauce
- ¼ tsp red pepper flakes
- ½ tsp garlic powder
- 1 tsp fresh chives, chopped

DIRECTIONS

1. Heat your oven in advance at 425°F.

2. Get a mixing container and in it mix the halved Brussels sprouts, garlic powder, red pepper flakes, bacon, buffalo sauce, and olive oil.

3. Add the freshly ground black pepper and the salt to season the mix.

4. Get a large baking sheet and cover it with the mixture evenly.

5. Place the large baking sheet into the oven you heated in advance and let it bake for 15 minutes when the bacon will be crispy and the Brussels sprouts tender.

6. Take the sheet out and use a wooden spoon to make six holes in the baked mixture.

7. Crack the eggs and pour in the holes you made using the wooden spoon and sprinkle a little freshly ground black pepper and salt to season the eggs.

8. Return the baking sheet to the oven and bake for 10 minutes until the eggs are done. Take the baking sheet out of the oven and sprinkle the fresh chives and buffalo sauce on top before serving.

LOW CARB BAGELS

NUTRINION

- Calories: 270
- Fat: 18 g
- Fiber: 1 g
- Carbohydrates: 3 g
- Protein: 22 g

PREPARATION TIME **10 MIN**   COOKING TIME **30 MIN**   SERVINGS **4**

INGREDIENTS

- 2 cups almond flour
- 3 tbsp bagel seasoning
- 1 tbsp baking powder
- 3 eggs
- 3 cups mozzarella cheese shredded
- ¼ cup cream cheese

DIRECTIONS

1. Heat your oven in advance at 400°F.

2. Get two baking sheets and line them well with paper made from parchment.

3. Get a large mixing container and mix in it the almond flour with the baking powder.

4. Mix the mozzarella cheese and the cream cheese in a bowl that can be used in a microwave. Place the bowl in a microwave for 2 minutes until the cheese melts and combines.

5. Get the mixture of cheese from the bowl once out of the microwave and pour it into the mixing container with the almond flour and the baking powder. Mix all the ingredients until well mixed.

6. Take the dough when done and divide it into eight parts that are equal in measure. Using your palms, take each of the eight dough parts and roll them into balls.

7. Using your fingers, create a hole in each of the balls, and gently stretch the dough to form the shape of a bagel.

8. Take one egg and beat it in a bowl. Brush the eggs on top of each made bagel following this by sprinkling the bagel seasoning at the top as well.

9. Place the bagel dough in the oven on its rack, which is in the middle for 25 minutes until they are nice and golden in color.

10. Remove the bagels from the oven and let them get cold for about 10 minutes before serving.

NUTRINION

- Calories: 350
- Fat: 8 g
- Fiber: 2 g
- Carbohydrates: 8 g
- Protein: 26 g

PREPARATION TIME **10 MIN**   COOKING TIME **20 MIN**   SERVINGS **1**

INGREDIENTS

- For the Tuna Cakes:
- ½ zucchini, grated
- 1 can drained tuna
- 2 tbsp oats
- 2 tbsp cheese of your choice, shredded
- 1 egg
- 0.24 tsp garlic salt
- 0.25 tsp dill
- 0.25 tsp onion powder
- Pepper to taste
- The Sauce:
- 2 tbsp yogurt, Greek-style is best
- 1 tsp juice of a lemon
- 0.25 tsp dill
- 0.25 tsp garlic salt

DIRECTIONS

1. Take a piece of cheesecloth, or similar and place the grated zucchini inside, twisting so that all the liquid comes out.

2. In a medium bowl, place the drained zucchini inside and add the tuna, oats, shredded cheese, garlic salt, dill, onion powder, pepper, and the egg, combining everything well.

3. Take a large frying pan and add a little olive oil, or cooking spray if you prefer.

4. Take half of the mixture and form a ball, before flattening it into a fish cake style, repeating with the other half.

5. Place the cakes into the frying pan, cooking over medium heat for around 6 minutes on each side.

6. Meanwhile, combine the sauce ingredients into a small mixing bowl and ensure they are mixed well.

7. Once the fish cakes are cooked place them on a serving plate and allow them to cool just slightly.

8. Add a spoonful of the sauce on top and enjoy!

QUICK RECIPES

LUNCH RECIPES

MEATY SPAGHETTI SQUASH

NUTRINION

- Calories: 210 kcal
- Fat: 12 g
- Fiber: 2 g
- Carbohydrates: 8 g
- Protein: 6 g

PREPARATION TIME **10 MIN**   COOKING TIME **50 MIN**   SERVINGS **6**

INGREDIENTS

- 1 egg
- 1 tsp oregano, dried
- 1 tsp basil, dried
- ¼ cup Parmesan cheese, grated
- ½ tsp salt
- 4 cups minced beef
- 1 tsp Worcestershire sauce
- 3 cups marinara sauce, low carb
- 2 cups mozzarella cheese, shredded
- 4 cups cooked low-carb spaghetti squash

DIRECTIONS

1. Heat your oven in advance at 250°F.

2. Take a mixing container and in it mix the minced beef, Worcestershire sauce, basil, oregano, egg, salt, and Parmesan cheese.

3. Take small scoops of the mix and make balls of meat taking care because they will be very soft.

4. Take a sheet used for baking and coat its bottom with a quarter cup of marinara sauce. Arrange the balls of meat you have prepared at the top then pour the remaining marinara sauce at the top coating all of them.

5. Place the sheet for baking in the oven you had heated in advance and let the balls of meat bake for half an hour until well cooked.

6. After half an hour, sprinkle the shredded mozzarella cheese on top of the baked balls of meat then replace it in the oven for the cheese to melt for about 3 minutes.

7. When all the cheese has melted, take them out of the oven and allow them to get cold completely before serving.

8. Take a plate and place in it the spaghetti squash and scoops of the baked balls of meat and enjoy.

CAJUN PORK SLIDERS

NUTRINION

- Calories: 382
- Fat: 22.4 g
- Fiber: 4.5 g
- Carbohydrates: 2.4 g
- Protein: 38.9 g

PREPARATION TIME **10 MIN**   COOKING TIME **45 MIN**   SERVINGS **4**

INGREDIENTS

- 4 low-carb bread slices
- 14 oz. pork loin
- 2 tbsp Cajun spices
- 1 tbsp olive oil
- 1/3 cup water
- 1 tsp tomato sauce

DIRECTIONS

1. Rub the pork loin with Cajun spices and place in the skillet.

2. Add olive oil and roast it over high heat for 5 minutes from each side.

3. After this, transfer the meat to the saucepan, and add tomato sauce and water.

4. Stir gently and close the lid.

5. Simmer the meat for 35 minutes.

6. Slice the cooked pork loin.

7. Place the pork sliders over the bread slices and transfer them to the serving plates.

LAMB CURRY

NUTRINION

- Calories: 181
- Fat: 9 g
- Fiber: 5 g
- Carbohydrates: 8 g
- Protein: 14 g

PREPARATION TIME **10 MIN**   COOKING TIME **4 H**   SERVINGS **6**

INGREDIENTS

- 2 tbsp fresh ginger, grated
- 2 garlic cloves, peeled and minced
- 2 tsp cardamom
- 1 onion, peeled and chopped
- 6 cloves
- 2 tomatoes
- 1 lb. lamb meat, cubed
- 2 tsp cumin powder
- 1 tsp garam masala
- ½ tsp chili powder
- 1 tsp turmeric
- 2 tsp coriander
- 1 lb. spinach
- 14 oz. canned

DIRECTIONS

1. In a slow cooker, mix lamb with tomatoes, spinach, ginger, garlic, onion, cardamom, cloves, cumin, garam masala, chili, turmeric, and coriander.

2. Stir well. Cover and cook on high for 4 hours.

3. Uncover the slow cooker, stir the chili, divide into bowls, and serve.

TURMERIC RACK OF LAMB

NUTRINION

- Calories: 252
- Fat: 18.8 g
- Fiber: 0.4 g
- Carbohydrates: 1.3 g
- Protein: 18.9 g

PREPARATION TIME **15 MIN**   COOKING TIME **15 MIN**   SERVINGS **4**

INGREDIENTS

- 13 oz. rack of lamb
- 1 tbsp ground turmeric
- ½ tsp chili flakes
- 3 tbsp olive oil
- 1 tbsp balsamic vinegar
- 1 tsp salt
- ½ tsp peppercorns
- ¾ cup water

DIRECTIONS

1. In a shallow bowl, mix up together ground turmeric, chili flakes, olive oil, balsamic vinegar, salt, peppercorns, and water.

2. Brush the rack of lamb with the oily mixture generously.

3. After this, preheat the grill to 380°F.

4. Place the rack of lamb on the grill and cook it for 8 minutes from each side.

5. The cooked rack of lamb should have a light crunchy crust.

BEEF SATAY WITH VEGETABLES

NUTRINION

- Calories: 191
- Fat: 9 g
- Fiber: 2 g
- Carbohydrates: 8 g
- Protein: 20 g

PREPARATION TIME **10 MIN**   COOKING TIME **50 MIN**

INGREDIENTS

- Flank steak cut into quarter-inch strips
- 2 tsp paste of Thai red curry
- ½ tsp fresh ginger ground
- ¼ cup coconut milk
- 1 tsp monk fruit sweetener granulated
- ¼ cup natural peanut butter
- 2 tsp low-sodium soy sauce
- 1 tsp lime juice
- 1 tsp extra-virgin olive oil
- 2 cauliflower heads, grated
- ¼ tsp salt
- ¼ tsp freshly ground powder of black pepper
- 1 cup green beans

DIRECTIONS

1. Heat an indoor grill in advance.

2. Get a container used for mixing and in it mix the milk from coconuts, natural peanut butter, soy sauce, monk fruit sweetener, Thai paste, and fresh ginger that has been ground.

3. Divide the above mix into two separate containers and in one, add the flank steak strips.

4. Let the flank steak marinate in the sauce for half an hour.

5. While waiting for the flank steak to marinate, take a frying skillet that is nonstick and add the extra-virgin olive oil to it.

6. When the oil is nice and hot, add the grated cauliflower together with black pepper that is freshly ground and salt to season it. Let this cook for 5 minutes.

7. Take the cooked cauliflower from the pan and in it, add some more olive oil, and fry the green beans for 5 minutes until they will appear to have a bright green color on them and are not too tender.

8. Take the marinated flanks of steak and grill them on an indoor grill you had heated in advance for about 3 minutes.

9. When ready, serve the grilled flanks of steak with the cooked cauliflower and green beans as well.

MINI THAI LAMB SALAD BITES

NUTRINION

- Calories: 58 kcal

- Fat: 2 g

- Fiber: 2 g

- Carbohydrates: 20 g

- Protein: 5 g

PREPARATION TIME **10 MIN**   COOKING TIME **8 MIN**   SERVINGS **15**

INGREDIENTS

- 1 large cucumber, cut into 0.39-inch thick diagonal rounds

- 0.55 lb. (250 g) Lamb Blackstrap

- ¾ cup cherry tomatoes quartered

- ⅓ cup fresh mint, loosely packed

- ⅓ cup fresh coriander, loosely packed

- ¼ small red onion, finely diced

- 1 tsp fish sauce

- Juice of 1 lime

- 1 tbsp Coconut oil

DIRECTIONS

1. Place a pan over medium heat and heat oil. Cook the lamb for 4 minutes on each side. Remove from heat and let it rest.

2. In a mixing bowl, toss the onions, tomatoes, mint, coriander, fish sauce, and lime juice.

3. Cut the lamb into thin strips and add to the salad bowl. Toss to combine.

4. Spoon an ample amount of mixture on each cucumber cut. Chill and serve.

BACON EGG AND SAUSAGE CUPS

NUTRINION

- Calories: 100 kcal
- Fat: 8 g
- Fiber: 2 g
- Carbohydrates: 20 g
- Protein: 5 g

PREPARATION TIME **10 MIN**   COOKING TIME **20 MIN**   SERVINGS **8**

INGREDIENTS

- 3 oz. breakfast sausages
- 2 bacon slices, chopped
- 4 large eggs
- 2 large green onions, chopped
- 1 oz. cheddar cheese, shredded
- 1 tbsp coconut oil

DIRECTIONS

1. Preheat the oven to 350°F.

2. Grease your muffin pan with coconut oil and set it aside.

3. In a mixing bowl, beat the eggs together with the cheese. Set aside.

4. Brown the bacon in a nonstick skillet over medium heat. Add the crumbled sausage and cook until no longer pink.

5. Add the onion and cook until wilted. Remove the skillet from the heat and let it cool for 1–2 minutes.

6. Add the meat mixture to the egg mixture and beat well using a spoon.

7. Scoop the mixture into the greased muffin pan and bake for 15–20 minutes or until the tops begin to brown. Remove from the pan and serve.

SMOKED SALMON AND AVOCADO STACKS

NUTRINION

- Calories: 106 kcal
- Fat: 12 g
- Fiber: 2 g
- Carbohydrates: 20 g
- Protein: 5 g

PREPARATION TIME **15 MIN**   COOKING TIME **0 MIN**   SERVINGS **6**

INGREDIENTS

- ½ lb. smoked salmon, finely diced
- 1 ripe avocado, seed removed and diced
- 1 tbsp chives, chopped
- Fresh or dried dill leaves for garnishing
- 3 tsp fresh lemon juice
- 2 tsp Black pepper, ground

DIRECTIONS

1. Combine salmon, chives, and 1 teaspoon of lemon juice in a small mixing bowl.

2. In another mixing bowl, toss the avocado, the remaining lemon juice, and pepper.

3. Using a presentation ring, arrange the stacks on the serving plates. Arrange the avocado at the bottom and top it with the salmon mixture and gently press. Remove the mold and garnish the stack with dill leaves. Serve chilled.

CINNAMON AND PECAN PORRIDGE

NUTRINION

- Calories: 580 kcal
- Fat: 42 g
- Fiber: 2 g
- Carbohydrates: 20 g
- Protein: 7 g

PREPARATION TIME **5 MIN**   COOKING TIME **10 MIN**   SERVINGS **2**

INGREDIENTS

- ½ tsp cinnamon
- ¼ cup pecans, chopped
- ¼ cup unsweetened coconut, toasted
- ¼ cup coconut milk
- ¼ cup almond butter
- ¾ cup unsweetened almond milk
- 1 tbsp extra-virgin coconut oil
- 2 tbsp hemp seeds
- 2 tbsp whole chia seeds

DIRECTIONS

1. Place a small saucepan over medium heat. Combine the coconut milk, coconut oil, almond butter, and almond milk. Bring to simmer and remove from heat.

2. Add the toasted coconut (leave some for the topping), cinnamon, pecans, hemp seeds, and chia seeds. Mix the ingredients well and allow resting for 5–10 minutes.

3. Divide between 2 bowls and serve.

SESAME-SEARED SALMON

NUTRINION

- Calories: 198 kcal

- Fat: 12 g

- Fiber: 2 g

- Carbohydrates: 20 g

- Protein: 5 g

PREPARATION TIME **5 MIN**   COOKING TIME **10 MIN**   SERVINGS **4**

INGREDIENTS

- 4 wild salmon fillets (about 1 lb.)

- 1 ½ tbsp sesame seeds

- 2 tbsp toasted sesame oil

- 1 ½ tbsp avocado oil

- 1 tsp sea salt

DIRECTIONS

1. Using a paper towel or a clean kitchen towel, pat the fillets to dry. Brush each with 1 tablespoon of sesame oil and season with ½ teaspoon of salt.

2. Place a large skillet over medium-high heat and drizzle with avocado oil. Once the oil is hot, add the salmon fillets with the flesh side down. Cook for about 3 minutes and flip. Cook the skin side for an additional 3–4 minutes without overcooking it.

3. Remove the pan from the heat and brush with the remaining sesame oil. Season with the remaining salt and sprinkle with sesame seeds. Best served with a green salad.

QUICK RECIPES

DINNER RECIPES

BUTTERNUT SQUASH RISOTTO

NUTRINION

- Calories: 337 kcal
- Fat: 25 g
- Carbohydrates: 9 g
- Protein: 8 g

PREPARATION TIME **10 MIN**   COOKING TIME **15 MIN**   SERVINGS **4**

INGREDIENTS

- 3 tbsp butter
- 2 tbsp minced sage
- ¼ tsp black pepper, ground
- 1 tsp minced rosemary
- 1 tsp salt
- ½ cup dry sherry
- 4 cups riced cauliflower
- ½ cup butternut squash, cooked and mashed
- ½ cup Parmesan cheese, grated
- ½ cup Mascarpone cheese
- ⅛ tsp grated nutmeg
- 1 tsp minced garlic

DIRECTIONS

1. Melt your butter inside of a large frying pan turned to a medium level of heat.
2. Add your rosemary, sage, and garlic. Cook this for about 1 minute or until this mixture begins to become fragrant.
3. Add the cauliflower rice, pepper, salt, and mashed squash. Cook this for 3 minutes. You will know it is ready for the next step when cauliflower starts to soften up.
4. Add your sherry and cook this for an additional 6 minutes, or until the majority of the liquid is absorbed into the rice, or when the cauliflower is much softer.
5. Stir in the Mascarpone cheese, Parmesan cheese, as well as nutmeg (grated).
6. Cook all of this on a medium heat level, being sure to stir it occasionally and do this until the cheese has melted and the risotto has gotten creamy. That will take around 4–5 minutes.
7. Taste the risotto and add more pepper and salt to season if you wish.
8. Remove your pan from the burner and garnish your risotto with more of the herbs as well as some grated Parmesan.
9. Serve and enjoy

CHEESY BROCCOLI SOUP

NUTRINION

- Calories: 97 kcal
- Fat: 3.6 g
- Carbohydrates: 13.4 g
- Protein: 5 g

PREPARATION TIME **5 MIN**   COOKING TIME **30 MIN**   SERVINGS **6**

INGREDIENTS

- 2 lb. broccoli, chopped
- Salt to taste
- 5 cup vegetable broth
- ¼ cup shredded cheddar cheese
- 1 tbsp olive oil
- ¼ cup lemon juice
- 2 garlic cloves, minced
- 1 white onion, chopped
- Pepper to taste

DIRECTIONS

1. Heat the olive oil in a pan with medium heat.

2. Fry the onion for 1 minute and then add the garlic. Fry until the garlic becomes golden in color.

3. Toss in the broccoli and stir for 3 minutes.

4. Pour in the vegetable broth.

5. Add salt and pepper and mix well.

6. Cook for 20 minutes or until your broccoli is entirely cooked through.

7. Take off the heat and let it cool down a bit.

8. Add to a blender, and blend it until your soup is perfectly smooth.

9. Transfer the soup into the pot again and heat it over medium heat.

10. Add lemon juice and cheddar cheese and check if it needs more seasoning.

11. Serve hot with more cheese on top.

BEEF CABBAGE STEW

NUTRINION

- Calories: 372 kcal
- Fat: 22.7 g
- Carbohydrates: 9 g
- Protein: 31.8 g

PREPARATION TIME 30MIN   **COOKING TIME 2 H**   **SERVINGS 8**

INGREDIENTS

- 2 lb. beef stew meat
- 1 cube beef bouillon
- 8 oz. tomato sauce
- ¼ cup chopped celery
- 2 bay leaves
- 8 oz. plum tomatoes, chopped
- 1 ⅓ cups hot chicken broth
- Salt and pepper to taste
- 1 cabbage
- 1 tsp Greek seasoning
- 4 onions, chopped

DIRECTIONS

1. Cut off the stem of the cabbage. Separate the leaves carefully. Wash well and rinse off. Set aside for now.

2. Fry the beef in a large pan over medium-low heat for about 8–10 minutes or until you get a brown color.

3. Into the pan, pour in ⅓ of the chicken broth.

4. Add the beef bouillon, and mix well.

5. Add the black pepper and salt and mix again.

6. Add the lid and cook on medium-low heat for about 1 hour.

7. Take off the heat and transfer the mix into a bowl.

8. Spread the cabbage leaves on a flat surface.

9. Fill the middle using the beef mixture. Use a generous portion of filling, and it will give your stew a better taste.

10. Wrap the cabbage leaves tightly. Use a kitchen thread to tie it. Finish it with the remaining leaves and filling.

11. In a pot, heat the oil and fry the onion for 1 minute.

12. Add the remaining chicken broth.

13. Add in the celery and tomato sauce and cook for another 10 minutes.

14. Add the Greek seasonings, and mix well. Bring to a boil, and then carefully add the wrapped cabbage.

15. Cover and cook for another 10 minutes.

16. Serve hot.

FRIED WHOLE TILAPIA

NUTRINION

- Calories: 368 kcal
- Fat: 30.1 g
- Carbohydrates: 9.2 g
- Protein: 16.6 g

PREPARATION TIME **10 MIN**   COOKING TIME **25 MIN**   SERVINGS **2**

INGREDIENTS

- 10 oz. tilapia
- 2 tbsp oil
- 4 large onions, chopped
- 2 garlic cloves, minced
- 2 tbsp red chili powder
- 1 tsp turmeric powder
- 1 tsp cumin powder
- 1 tsp coriander powder
- Salt to taste
- Black pepper to taste
- 2 tbsp soy sauce
- 2 tbsp fish sauce

DIRECTIONS

1. Take the tilapia fish and clean it well without taking off the skin. You need to fry it whole, so you have to be careful about cleaning the gut inside.

2. Cut a few slits on the skin, so the seasoning gets inside well.

3. Marinate the fish with fish sauce, soy sauce, red chili powder, garlic, cumin powder, turmeric powder, coriander powder, salt, and pepper.

4. Coat half of the onions in the same mixture too.

5. Let them marinate for 1 hour.

6. In a skillet, heat the oil. Fry the fish for 8 minutes on each side.

7. Transfer the fish to a serving plate.

8. Fry the marinated onions until they become crispy.

9. Add the remaining raw onions on top and serve hot.

AFRICAN CHICKEN CURRY

NUTRINION

- Calories: 354 kcal
- Fat: 10 g
- Protein: 18 g
- Carbohydrates: 17 g

PREPARATION TIME **10 MIN**   COOKING TIME **30 MIN**   SERVINGS **4**

INGREDIENTS

- 1 lb. whole chicken
- ½ onion
- ½ cup coconut milk
- ½ bay leaf
- 1 ½ tsp olive oil
- ½ cup peeled tomatoes
- 1 tsp curry powder
- ⅛ tsp salt
- ½ lemon, juiced
- 1 garlic clove

DIRECTIONS

1. Keep the skin of the chicken.

2. Cut your chicken into 8 pieces. It looks good when you keep the size not too small or not too big.

3. Discard the skin of the onion and garlic and mince the garlic and dice the onion.

4. Cut the tomato wedges.

5. Now, in a pot, add the olive oil and heat over medium heat.

6. Add the garlic and fry until it becomes brown.

7. Add the diced onion and caramelize it.

8. Add the bay leaf and chicken pieces.

9. Fry the chicken pieces until they are golden.

10. Add the curry powder, coconut milk, and salt.

11. Cover and cook for 10 minutes on high heat.

12. Lower the heat to medium-low and add the lemon juice.

13. Add the tomato wedges.

14. Cook for another 10 minutes.

15. Serve hot with rice or tortilla.

YUMMY GARLIC CHICKEN LIVERS

NUTRINION

- Calories: 174 kcal
- Fat: 9 g
- Protein: 18 g
- Carbohydrates: 2.4 g

PREPARATION TIME **10 MIN**   COOKING TIME **30 MIN**   SERVINGS **2**

INGREDIENTS

- ½ lb. chicken liver
- 6 garlic cloves, minced
- ½ tsp salt
- 1 tbsp ginger garlic paste
- 1 cup diced onion
- 1 tbsp red chili powder
- 1 tsp cumin
- 1 tsp coriander powder
- Black pepper to taste
- 1 cardamom
- 2 tomatoes
- 1 cinnamon stick
- 1 bay leaf
- 4 tbsp olive oil
- 2 tbsp lemon juice
- 1 tbsp water

DIRECTIONS

1. In a large pan, heat your oil over high heat.

2. Add the garlic and fry until golden brown.

3. Add onion and fry until they become caramelized.

4. Turn the heat to medium and add the bay leaf, cinnamon stick, and cardamom, and toss for 30 seconds.

5. Add the ginger-garlic paste and 1 tablespoon of water. Adding water prevents burning.

6. Add the coriander powder, black pepper, salt, cumin, and red chili powder.

7. Cover and cook for 3 minutes on low heat.

8. Add the livers and 2 tablespoons of lemon juice and cook on medium heat for 15 minutes.

9. Add the tomatoes and cook for another 5 minutes.

10. Check the seasoning. Add more salt if needed.

11. Serve hot with a tortilla.

HEALTHY CHICKPEA BURGER

NUTRINION

- Calories: 254 kcal
- Fat: 12 g
- Protein: 9 g
- Carbohydrates: 7.8 g

PREPARATION TIME **15 MIN**   COOKING TIME **10 MIN**   SERVINGS **2**

INGREDIENTS

- 1 cup chickpeas, boiled
- 1 tbsp tomato puree
- 1 tsp soy sauce
- A pinch paprika
- A pinch white pepper
- 1 onion, diced
- Salt to taste
- 2 lettuce leaves
- ½ cup bell pepper, sliced
- 1 tsp olive oil
- 1 avocado, sliced
- 2 burger buns to serve

DIRECTIONS

1. Mash the chickpeas and combine them with bell pepper, salt, pepper, paprika, soy sauce, and tomato puree.

2. Use your hands to make patties.

3. Fry the patties until golden brown with oil.

4. Assemble the burgers with lettuce, onion, and avocado, and enjoy.

QUINOA PROTEIN BARS

NUTRINION

- Calories: 269 kcal
- Carbohydrates: 30 g
- Fat: 15 g
- Protein: 6 g

PREPARATION TIME **15 MIN**   COOKING TIME **45 MIN**   SERVINGS **16**

INGREDIENTS

- ½ cup almonds, chopped
- ½ cup chocolate chips
- ½ cup coconut oil, melted
- ½ cup flaxseed, ground
- ½ cup honey
- ½ tsp salt
- 1 cup quinoa, dry
- 2 ¼ cups quick oats
- 3 large egg whites

DIRECTIONS

1. Preheat the oven to 325°F.

2. On the bottom of a clean, dry baking sheet, evenly spread oats, quinoa, and almonds.

3. Bake for about 15 minutes or until lightly brown. You may want to stir the items in the cookie sheet every few minutes to ensure nothing burns.

4. Remove the grains and nuts from the oven and allow cooling completely, but don't turn off the oven.

5. Whisk the egg whites in a bowl and beat the coconut oil and honey into them.

6. Combine flaxseed, chocolate chips, and salt into the cooled grains and nuts, and then pour it into the mixing bowl, coating everything completely.

7. Line your baking sheet with parchment paper and spread the mixture evenly onto it, pressing it into one even layer. You may want to shape the sides of the mass, depending on whether or not it reaches the edges of your baking sheet without thinning out too much.

8. Bake for 30 minutes, and then remove from the oven.

9. Let cool for 1 hour before slicing into evenly-shaped bars, then cool completely.

10. Enjoy!

SOUTHWEST CHICKEN SALAD

NUTRINION

- Calories: 217 kcal
- Carbohydrates: 30 g
- Fat: 9 g
- Protein: 7 g

PREPARATION TIME 15 MIN   COOKING TIME 0 MIN   SERVINGS 8

INGREDIENTS

- ¼ cup extra-virgin olive oil
- ¼ cup red onion, finely chopped
- 1 cup corn, drained
- 1 can low-sodium black beans, rinsed and drained
- 1 jalapeño, seeded and minced
- 1 tsp chili powder
- 1 tsp cumin
- 1 tsp garlic powder
- 1 tsp onion powder
- 2 bell peppers, diced
- 2 large limes, juiced
- 2 lb. chicken thighs, cooked and diced
- 2 tbsp cilantro, finely chopped
- 3 cups quinoa, cooked
- Sea salt and black pepper, to taste

DIRECTIONS

1. In a small bowl, mix chili powder, lime juice, onion powder, garlic powder, cumin, and cilantro. Mix thoroughly and set aside.

2. In a large mixing bowl, combine all other ingredients and toss until thoroughly combined.

3. Drizzle seasoning mixture over the salad and toss to coat thoroughly.

4. Cover and refrigerate for 30 minutes before serving.

TUNA SALAD

NUTRINION

- Calories: 152 kcal
- Carbohydrates: 2 g
- Fat: 8 g
- Protein: 18 g

PREPARATION TIME **15 MIN**   COOKING TIME **0 MIN**   SERVINGS **10**

INGREDIENTS

- ¼ cup mayonnaise
- ¼ cup red onion, finely diced
- ¾ cup plain yogurt
- 1 garlic clove, minced
- 1 large stalk celery, diced
- 1 tbsp lemon juice
- 2 small dill pickles, diced
- 24 oz. tuna packed in water, drained
- Sea salt and pepper, to taste

DIRECTIONS

1. In a medium bowl, thoroughly mix all ingredients.

2. Chill in the fridge for 12 minutes while covered before serving.

3. Serve chilled!

CONCLUSION

Many people have found benefits from fasting, no matter their age. Women, in particular, may feel that they will not lose weight or be able to stick with the diet. They might even hear the criticism of other women who are doing it: "You're too old to be doing this!"

In reality, intermittent fasting can help you lose weight, have more energy, and gain a better connection with your body. Women over the age of 50 find it easier to fast than men of the same age because they have a lower risk of health complications and do not lose as much muscle mass while fasting as men do. There are two different forms of intermittent fasting suitable for women over 50, known as the 16:8 method and the 5:2 method.

In the 16:8 method, you fast for 16 hours and then only eat for 8 hours. You can break up the fasting period in any way that works best for your schedule. For example, you could choose to stop eating at 8 pm and start eating again at 12 pm. This will require a lot of discipline at first because it is hard to go that long without food!

If you're just getting started with intermittent fasting, this is a great place to start. To stay within your recommended daily intake, you should keep track of your calories even when you aren't eating.

In the 5:2 method, you fast for two days a week. For example, you would eat whatever you wanted on Monday and then eat very little on Tuesday and Wednesday.

The key is to eat as little as possible on non-fasting days so that your body can burn fat while you sleep without having to worry about digestion. You should drink lots of water before bed to help with sleep and dehydration. Five days out of the week, it is recommended that you consume carbohydrates after exercising or at night before going to bed to replenish muscle glycogen.

Another benefit of this method is that it can help women with irregular cycles have more regular periods. However, if you are going to try this method, slowly transition to it starting on the day of the fast. By taking the first 24 hours off from eating, to begin with, you will be able to better regulate your period so that it doesn't become irregular.

A lot of people say that this should only be done once or twice a year, but for some women, it can work year-round because the effect is cumulative on your metabolism. After about three months of fasting, many women will start losing at least 10 pounds.

When you cut calories, your body will start to consume adipose tissue. You should be prepared for a reduction in energy levels because this is the time when women will start to feel hungry. Just remember that you aren't doing this so that you can eat a lot; you are doing it so that you can be healthy and lose weight.

As soon as enough adipose tissue has been burned off, you will notice an improvement in your energy levels and endurance. During the fast, try to move around for at least 20 minutes a day, but do not exercise because that will break the fast too quickly. Yoga is usually the best exercise for women who are just starting with fasting since it doesn't involve doing anything too vigorous.

Your body will start to adapt to eating less on day eight of fasting. Once your body has adjusted, you should be able to maintain your weight loss and have healthy periods.

Made in the USA
Monee, IL
27 August 2022

12529411R00077